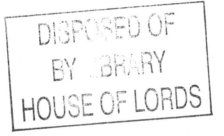

AGENDA FOR SOCIAL DEMOCRACY

Essays on the prospects for
new economic thinking and policy
in the changing British political scene

ARTHUR SELDON   RALPH HARRIS
GEOFFREY E. WOOD   A. R. PREST
MICHAEL BEENSTOCK   S. C. LITTLECHILD
LJUBO SIRC   CHARLES K. ROWLEY
A. I. MacBEAN

Published by
THE INSTITUTE OF ECONOMIC AFFAIRS
1983

Hobart Paperback No. 15

First published in May 1983 by
THE INSTITUTE OF ECONOMIC AFFAIRS
2 Lord North Street, Westminster,
London SW1P 3LB

ISSN 0309-1783
ISBN 0-255 36162-9

Printed in England by
Goron Pro-Print Co. Ltd., Lancing, West Sussex
Text set in Monotype Times Roman 11 on 12pt.

CONTENTS

Economic aspects of public policy – The meaning
of 'social democracy' – Productivity, equality,
equity – A new enlightenment: state and market –
Exchange in the market or mutual aid outside it

The inadequacy of good intentions – The age of
inflation – Trade union irresponsibility – The
Rake's progress – Macro-government *v.* micro-
markets – Seeds of decline – Unleashing the vote
motive – Three imperatives for social democracy –
Limits of government – A challenge to the 'mould
breakers'

NINE:

BRITAIN'S INTERNATIONAL
ECONOMIC POLICY   149

A. I. MacBean

PREFACE

This collection of essays is the outcome of a suggestion made by Professor A. R. Prest at a discussion of the Institute's past and future work during a meeting of its Advisers. The proposal was that, in view of the emergence of 'social democracy' as an apparently new approach to public policy, and more specifically in the formation of a new political party, we should indicate the approach of economists to the economics of social democracy whether as the emerging and still forming policy of the new party or as a collection of economic approaches to specific issues found in all parties, such as public finance, the structure of industry, industrial relations, welfare services, international economic relations, and so on.

Economists were invited to contribute essays written primarily by them as economic analysts without necessarily evincing either uncritical sympathy or over-sceptical hostility. It is in this spirit that they have been written with the purpose of elucidating the implications of what is being said and thought, or re-thought, by Social Democrats and by social democrats who can be found in all parties with other labels.

The first essay is an expansion of notes circulated to authors indicating the issues we hoped they would cover in their texts. The second is a review of the post-war economic scene and the problems it has yielded to be solved by people in any party likely to form British governments in the years ahead.

May 1983   ARTHUR SELDON

ONE

NEW HOPE FOR ECONOMIC POLICY IN A CHANGING POLITY

Arthur Seldon

The Author

ARTHUR SELDON: has been associated with the IEA since 1957. Editorial Director until 1981. Founder-Editor of the *Journal of Economic Affairs*. Founder-Trustee, Social Affairs Unit. Member, Board of Advisers, *The Journal of Post-Misesian Economics*. Member of the board of the Mont Pèlérin Society. His most recent publications are *Corrigible Capitalism, Incorrigible Socialism* (IEA Occasional Paper 57, 1980), and *Wither the Welfare State* (IEA Occasional Paper 60, 1981). Forthcoming essay, 'The New Economics', to be published in *The Journal of Social, Political and Economic Studies* (George Mason University, Spring 1983). He is working on several books.

New Hope for Economic Policy in a Changing Polity

The IEA has for many years been interested not only in the analysis of economic thought but also in the processes which decide whether and how economic thinking is translated into policy. This is the purpose for which the *Hobart Paperbacks* were established in 1971. The first volume was written by the distinguished British economist, Professor W. H. Hutt, under the title *Politically Impossible . . .?*, to set the tone for the whole series. Since the Institute had found in its early years that promising new thinking had been pre-judged and prematurely discouraged by the assurance of 'practical men' that it was 'politically impossible', the determination to pursue economic thinking rigorously to its logical conclusions has pervaded the work of the IEA since its foundation in 1957.

This attitude—that the duty of economists was to stick to their last and not to think as politicians—has been amply vindicated by events. Some of the ideas in early IEA Papers that seemed to have little chance of adoption when first analysed have lately become the currency not only of economic debate but also of political discussion in Parliament and in the media. Some have been incorporated in policy, for example in the abolition of exchange control, the shift to floating exchange rates and the abandonment of incomes policies. Others have at last breached conventional thinking, not least on education, health, housing, pen-

3

sions and income maintenance. The objection 'politi-cally impossible' has now become particularly irrelevant in the last two or three years.

The long-delayed re-orientation within the British political parties began with the Labour Party, con-tinued through the Alliance between the Social Demo-cratic and Liberal Parties and may proceed to the Conservative Party. The result has been to open up new readiness to consider as potential public policy economic thinking on the scope for the market, quasi-market and other voluntary institutions that has too long lain dormant, despised and rejected by public men who did not understand its wide and deep implications for equity and harmony as well as efficiency. I discuss these implications and the scope for new policies below.

Economic aspects of public policy

The essays assembled in *Hobart Paperback 15* under the title *Agenda for Social Democracy* were written on seven main policies by independent professional econ-omists. They follow a review by Lord Harris of the post-war economic scene and the all-party policies that failed to solve its dilemmas, not least to combine efficiency with humanity.

The essays are addressed to people in public, aca-demic, industrial and other activities, not as members of political parties but as people who wish to combine what have hitherto seemed to be, or at least have been said to be, irreconcilable objectives—dominantly, econ-omic freedom and social equity. All the contributors are interested in showing what the specialist expertise in their subject can contribute to the discussion— Geoffrey Wood on inflation and the labour market,

Professor A. R. Prest on taxation, Professor Michael Beenstock on social policy, Professor S. C. Littlechild on competition, Dr Ljubo Sirc on employee participation, Professor A. I. MacBean on international policy, and, not least, and in a sense fundamental to all, Professor C. K. Rowley on the formation of economic policy as seen through the school of public choice economists who analyse the working of government and its motivations as economists have long analysed industry.

The economists are therefore all interested in discussing economic policy for social democracy as a policy, not necessarily of one Party. Some show a measure of sympathy for SDP and Alliance thinking and prospects in particular, but they write primarily as scholars and their main aim is to discern conflicts between analysis and policy, economic means and economic ends. Thus, Professor Littlechild agrees with much of the SDP approach to the maintenance of competition, but suggests that its current thinking could with advantage be revised to make its objective more certain.

As always the main purpose of the Institute is to show the light that economic analysis can shed on current thought and policy in all schools and parties in the realm. It is not concerned with the direction from which practical or Parliamentary interest is forthcoming, but has persevered with its function of following economic analysis wherever it leads and making its work available to all who wish to explore below surface rhetoric or rise above popular sentiment.

These essays are timely because the contemporary political re-alignment—the emergence in Britain of 'social democracy' in the overt form of a new political party and its alliance with an older party—is significant for economic policy and the contribution to it of economic science. For it indicates a candid recognition of past errors in policy by statesmen and politicians and in economic thinking by academics. It therefore promises a more ready approach to underlying truth than in the years of Conservative-Labour 'duopoly' when it was concealed by over-expectations from the power of myopic government and under-estimation of the beneficent power of market forces in shaping the economy and society.

The meaning of 'social democracy'

The term 'social democracy' can be understood in several senses. For economists, interest lies in its expression of a desire to combine the strengths of four elements in evolving the good society: first, the decentralised market, with all it implies in local, voluntary or mutual co-operation in private activity and enterprise; second, profit as the reward of entrepreneurship; third, pricing as the method of rationing scarce resources between alternative uses; and, not least, fourth, the 'social justice' of common access to the means of civilised living. 'Social democracy' with these ingredients thus hopes to reconcile the economic efficiency necessary for high living standards with the sense of equity and humanity desirable for communal harmony.

In this sense 'social democracy' is not new to British public life or political institutions. For part of British history in the 19th century, the critics of liberal capitalism said that efficiency was given precedence over equality or humanity: living standards rose rapidly but not uniformly, so that wealth co-existed with wide inequalities and poverty. Between the two world wars, wealth advanced further despite the early restrictions on markets and 'the great depression', but poverty, conspicuous inequalities and insecurity in sickness, unemployment and old age persisted.

Productivity, equality, equity

Concern about the 'social' consequences of rapid change in the 19th- and early 20th-century conditions of supply and demand and of the 10-year 'trade cycle' were the common property of public men in all the historical political parties—Conservative, Labour and Liberal—whether their reactions or motivations were emotional, intellectual or predominantly electoral—or a mixture of all three. Since 'social justice' was furthered by increases in production as a prelude to re-distribution, they differed in their judgement of the extent to which technological change and social advance could be retarded in order to minimise inequalities without prejudicing the general progress of the economy and the rise in the living standards of all, even if shared unequally. But the desire to reconcile progress with humanity has moved British public men and government of all political parties and scholars of all schools because it expresses national sentiment over two centuries. It is not a new development in the 1980s, but a new turn in national concern by the more fortunate for the less fortunate and a readiness to contemplate new and more effective methods of reconciling progress with liberty and liberty with humanity.

What is new in the thinking in all parties and schools is the change in the understanding of the economic institutions required to attain the optimum combination of economic advance and 'social justice'. For 200 years the classical British liberal thinking has been that the open society was, with unhampered access to resources and scientific method in free or quasi markets, the best vehicle for productivity and the removal of poverty. For 100 years since the 1880s the Fabians have taught that government, national and municipal, is the essential instrument of both efficiency and humanity. For 50 years the self-styled followers of J. M. Keynes have taught that government can ensure high output through full employment without inflation by 'managing' the national demand for goods and services. For 40 years the followers of Beveridge and Titmuss have taught that only government can reduce or remove the inequalities, injustices and poverty accompanying economic freedom even where it produces progress.

Thus the significant new element in the 1980s is the questioning of this efficacy of the state by influential public men and women who had accepted it for 30 or 40 years of political activity or power in government. Without abandoning their emphasis on equity or humanity, more leaders and thinkers in all parties, Conservative, Liberal, Social Democratic and, to a larger degree than is made public, Labour, now believe it cannot be assured by the centralising state, that government has been allowed too much control of economic life to the point of endangering both prosperity and liberty. So much for the 'consensus' on the limitations of government. But, perhaps more unexpectedly, yet for that reason more hopefully, there is increasing assertion that the prosperity required to sustain humanity and abolish poverty requires increased use of decentralised institutions based on individual, group, local initiatives, voluntary, mutual, competitive or commercial, that reflect better knowledge of local circumstances, family preferences and individual aspirations. This change in emphasis is heard most from some leaders, academics and rank-and-file in the Conservative and Social Democratic Parties.

A new enlightenment: state and market

In this attitude to the requirements for maximum production and optimal re-distribution, the pursuit of prosperity and equality, the reconciliation of efficiency and humanity, and consequently the relative rôles of the state and the market, economists who see virtue in the market and other voluntary decentralised institutions may re-appraise and re-assert their relevance and scope in answering questions that must be answered in what may now be hoped will be a new enlightenment following disillusionment with the state and its far-reaching agencies in nationalised industry, transport, fuel and welfare, and in local authority jurisdiction over much of private and family life.

1. What is the combination of the necessary functions of government and the maximum scope for voluntary exchange in the market or in co-operative or mutual activity that will promote the optimal reconciliation of efficiency and equity?

2. How far has equality been pursued at the expense of progress and without benefit to the relatively poor? And, as a corollary: How far do the still relatively poor prefer equality or less poverty?

3. How far may it be easier to remove by re-distributed taxation or other measures differences in income or wealth that decide access to goods and services in the open market than to remove by

political activism or 'participation' differences in cultural, occupational or political power that decide access to services supplied by the state?

4. How far can equalisation of opportunity be achieved indirectly by removing obstacles to mobility, exchange and co-operation as well as by direct re-distribution of income?

5. How much inequality and even inequity is the necessary price that has to be paid for progress in a dynamic, innovative, flexible economy? What are the lessons of East as well as West Europe?

6. How far can government, central or local, relax the dispensable control of economic activity beyond the supply of joint, collective 'public' goods.

7. Is it sufficient to decentralise government politically to regional or local authorities elected in the ballot box, or must it proceed further to enable individuals or groups to control producers more effectively by the power to withhold their purchasing power in the market?

8. How much of the British economy can be controlled by government or must be left to the market or other independent institutions in an increasingly interdependent world linked by trade and investment? If 60 per cent is too large, how soon can it be reduced to 50 per cent? How urgent is it to reach 40 per cent?

9. How can the cultural attachment to 'security', embodied and crystallised in the welfare state, be reconciled with the necessity to adapt British insti-

tutions to a continually evolving world with accelerating technical innovation and social advance?

10. Not least, how can the transition, where desirable, from the state to the market and voluntary institutions be made with least dislocation and most harmony by removing the power of politicians, officials and trade unions to obstruct reform in central and local government?

Exchange in the market or mutual aid outside it

These are among the main questions, addressed in brief to the contributors to this book, that will be faced in the 1980s and 1990s by politicians in all parties who have in recent years increasingly recognised the essential rôles of decentralised markets and other voluntary organisations in reconciling high productivity with spreading opportunities, efficiency with humanity—Messrs Roy Jenkins, David Owen, William Rodgers, Dick Taverne, John Horam and others among the Social Democrats, Messrs Jo Grimond, John Pardoe, Richard Wainwright and others among the Liberals, Mrs Margaret Thatcher, Sir Keith Joseph, Sir Geoffrey Howe, Messrs Norman Tebbit, David Howell, Nigel Lawson and others among the Conservatives. In this sense they are all 'social democrats'. And if it comes to pass that the British Government to the end of the century and beyond alternates between two political coalitions, both of which accept the verdict of history that voluntary co-operation, in the market or outside it, is not only compatible with social equity but essential to achieve it, the British economy may re-emerge to rejoin the industrial leaders of the world in whose countries there has been both more rapid economic progress and increasing equality of opportunity and income in thriving decentralised and spontaneous economic activity.

The essays in this collection are intended as a contribution to re-thinking among men and women in British public life. They are addressed to 'social democrats' in all parties, to teachers and students of economics who will be a major influence in the ferment of policy reform until the end of the century and beyond, and to people in all walks of life concerned with the translation of ideas into policy in their lifetimes.

TWO

THE MOULD TO BE BROKEN

Ralph Harris

The Author

RALPH HARRIS: born in 1924, educated at Tottenham Grammar School and Queen's College, Cambridge. He was Lecturer in Political Economy at St Andrews University, 1949-56, and has been General Director of the Institute of Economic Affairs since 1957. He wrote (with Arthur Seldon) *Hire Purchase in a Free Society*, *Advertising in a Free Society*, *Choice in Welfare*, etc., for the IEA. His essay, 'In Place of Incomes Policy', was published in *Catch '76 . . .?* (Occasional Paper 'Special' (No. 47), 1976). His most recent works are *The End of Government . . .?*, which consisted of two public lectures and speeches delivered in the House of Lords (Occasional Paper 58, 1980), and with Arthur Seldon, *Pricing or Taxing?* (Hobart Paper No. 71, 1976), *Not from Benevolence . . .* (Hobart Paperback No. 10, 1977), and *Over-ruled on Welfare* (Hobart Paperback No. 13, 1979); and he contributed the Epilogue, 'Can Confrontation be Avoided?', to *The Coming Confrontation* (Hobart Paperback No. 12, 1978).

He is a Trustee of the Wincott Foundation and Secretary of the Political Economy Club, formerly Secretary, now President, of the Mont Pèlérin Society, and a Council Member of Buckingham University.

Ralph Harris was created a Life Peer in July 1979 as Lord Harris of High Cross.

The Mould to be Broken

How can we in the West explain the cruel descent from post-war hopes for prosperity, full employment and stable prices to the present grim realities of pervasive stagnation, unemployment and inflation? The mutual accusations of party men and their academic apologists offer no illumination. Throughout Europe governments variously labelled Conservative, Socialist, Liberal, Christian or Social Democrat have all contributed unwittingly to the process of collective disillusionment and confusion. The national records of failure have varied only in pace and extent.

The inadequacy of good intentions
The most striking common feature in countries as different as Sweden, Germany and Britain has been the apparent conflict between the professed good intentions of politicians and their increasingly disappointing collective attainments. Policies pursued in the name of the 'public interest' have everywhere led to spreading public disaffection and rejection in the polling booth or black economy. More specifically, the almost single-minded devotion to economic security has been mocked by the spectre of rising prices and declining prospects for employment.

If this failure of governments cannot be attributed to want of trying, neither can it be blamed on lack of legal or fiscal power by politicians to impose their will.

Indeed, the apparent authority of politicians over national economies has throughout the post-war years everywhere been remorselessly extended. In the name of the 'mixed economy', a growing share of spending, employment and output has been brought under the direct control of government and its agencies, to say nothing of the extension of regulation and control over what is left of private production and consumption.

This ruling consensus has shifted cumulatively in a collectivist direction, as the active pressure from more socialist governments has alternated in most countries with the acquiescence of less socialist governments to produce the familiar ratchet effect we have seen in Britain under the banner of 'Butskellism'.[1] When the policies of many independent countries governed by parties with differing aims follow so broadly similar a course, it is natural to seek a common influence. It can hardly be doubted that the twin influences that dominated economic policy in Europe and beyond after 1945 were, firstly, the ideas associated with the name of J. M. Keynes, and, secondly, the false repute won by 'planning' in the single-minded waging of war, which led to the unfounded assumption that governments could redirect national production towards the wholly different, because diverse, pursuit of peaceful prosperity.

The age of inflation

For the politicians, sometimes as anxious to do good as to win votes, the simple message divined (without reading) from the 400 pages of Keynes's *General Theory*

---

[1] A term coined in the 1950s to indicate the broadly shared approach of Hugh Gaitskell (Labour) and R. A. Butler (Conservative) who succeeded him in 1951 as Chancellor of the Exchequer.

of Employment, Interest and Money[2] was that by suitable manipulation of government spending and taxation total demand for national output could be stimulated to provide 'jobs for all'. So it was that in 1945 a Labour Government committed to planning had no hesitation in pledging itself to 'full employment'. This quickly came to be interpreted as justifying a stimulus to national spending whenever unemployment looked like rising above 350,000 in a large and diverse labour force of more than 20 million producing goods and services of which around one-third were exported to almost every country in the world. Was this really what Keynes meant, as his followers endlessly claim?

Certainly while Keynes could still speak for himself he leant against the more ambitious targets for 'full employment'. In 1937, when the Chancellor had proposed additional spending of £80 million (about 1·5 per cent of GNP) on re-armament, Keynes had written to *The Times* (11 March) about the danger of inflation although unemployment stood above 1·5 million or about 10 per cent of the insured labour force (now equivalent to 2·5 million). Likewise, even during the euphoria of war, Keynes had opposed the 3 per cent target popularised by Beveridge in the book Professor Sir Dennis Robertson always miscalled '*Free* Employment in a *Full* Society'. It was Robertson who pointed out that only after Keynes had died did politicians come to regard unemployment of 2 per cent 'almost as a symptom of the end of the world'.

Whatever the technical merits of the economic analysis advanced by Keynes in his extensive and often contradictory writings, it was the political influence of the self-styled Keynesians which has undoubtedly been

[2] Macmillan, 1936.

responsible for the recent unparalleled combination of inflation and unemployment. In their remarkable book, *Democracy in Deficit*, Professors James Buchanan and Richard Wagner expressed the charge as follows:

> 'Keynesian economics has turned the politicians loose; it has destroyed the effective constraint on politicians' ordinary appetites [to] spend and spend without the apparent necessity to tax.'[3]

To set the resulting Age of Inflation in its historical context, Professor Ivor Pearce has calculated[4] that in the seven centuries since the year 1300 the general price level of comparable goods has risen 300-fold and that of this currency debasement 96 per cent has taken place since Keynes wrote *The General Theory* in 1936.

Trade union irresponsibility

It is not only in Britain that Keynesian 'full employment' policy has provided a recipe for monetary incontinence which produced accelerating inflation and put party political allegiances under increasing strain. All democracies have proved vulnerable to similar pressures from what Sir William Rees-Mogg has called 'a great burst of inordinacy'.[5] But if Britain has paid a higher price than most formerly stable Western societies the major blame rests with our still uniquely-privileged, legally-protected trade unions.

As economists have long understood and Keynes acknowledged, unemployment can arise from a wide variety of changes, whether originating in consumer

[3] Academic Press, New York and London, 1977, p. 4.

[4] Quoted in the *Sunday Telegraph*, 6 June 1982, and summarised in graphic form in Peter Smith, 'Inflation Before and After Keynes', *Journal of Economic Affairs*, Vol. 3, No. 3, April 1983.

[5] *The Reigning Error*, Hamish Hamilton, 1974.

demand, foreign trade, new products or innovation in techniques of production. Ceaseless shifts in the composition of national output are an indispensable companion of economic progress. Employment cannot be static but has constantly to be renewed. It requires a continual movement of labour from old, declining employments into new, expanding industries and services. The resulting disturbance to familiar ways of working inevitably brings short-term discomfort. Faced with such changes, British unions sought to preserve old jobs by resisting adaptations that were indispensable for long-term prosperity.

For more than a hundred years—and in as many ways—British trade unions have institutionalised the natural, human resistance to change. Instead of seeking security and economic progress, as in Japan, by extracting from efficient employers the best terms for responding flexibly to new machines in different locations, they have more often pursued the mirage of security by deploying increasingly irresistible coercion to impose over-manning, phoney overtime, demarcation, long apprenticeships, short measure at work, closed shops and control over entry. At the same time, through their control over the Labour Party, British trade union leaders have been able to extend policies of nationalisation, rent control, subsidised council housing, ever-increasing welfare, so-called employment protection, higher taxation, and other brakes on mobility, adaptation, efficiency and risk-taking, including the squeezing of profits on which lasting employment depends.

For strong trade unions, Keynesian 'full employment' policy was an invitation to irresponsibility. So long as the government stood ready to fend off unemployment by inflating the currency to stimulate demand, both unions and management came to understand that unearned wage increases could be largely passed on in higher prices borne up on a rising tide of inflation. Such collusion was especially rife in pampered 'public' industries and corporations that are sheltered from competition, for example in fuel and transport, local government, education and medical care—still most vulnerable to damaging strikes for unrealistic wage claims.

The Rake's progress

The outcome of this combination of monetary laxity and strong union pressure can be summarised briefly. Inflation started creeping at 2-3 per cent a year in the 1950s, speeded up to 5-8 per cent in the 1960s, and galloped at 10-25 per cent in the 1970s. Unemployment, which had been 'fine-tuned' around 350,000 after 1945, never fell below 500,000 after 1967, rose towards 1·5 million under Labour in the mid-1970s and by 1982 doubled to 3 million in the official statistics. To put the story more baldly, larger injections of monetary demand yielded a diminishing effect on employment and an increasing impact on the price level. The Rake's progress is brought home by comparing two 5-year periods. Thus over the last five Macmillan years of 1959-64, an increase in nominal national income (or total spending) of 38 per cent reflected a 19 per cent increase in output and a 15 per cent rise in prices. Over the last five Wilson-Callaghan years of 1974-79, an increase in total spending of almost 13 per cent brought a rise in output of 9 per cent while prices rose by 109 per cent.[6] It is no wonder that 1979 appears to be a water-

[6] A fuller account of the changing relationship between spending, employment and inflation will be found in the outstanding Hobart Paper 90 by Samuel Brittan, entitled *How to End the 'Monetarist' Controversy*, IEA, Second Edition, 1982.

shed for political allegiances visible both in the divided Conservative Party and in the fracture of the Labour Party by the creation of the Social Democratic Party.

The main reason for this worsening performance was the fading of the 'money illusion' that average prices could be assumed to remain broadly stable. The more people came to anticipate inflation, the less effect Keynesian monetary expansion had on real magnitudes like output or employment, and the more effect it had on such nominal components as wages and prices.

The full cost of the Keynesian consensus for rising prices and, ultimately, unemployment was obscured so long as the Bretton Woods system of fixed exchange rates remained more or less intact. Thus, when British prices rose faster than our competitors', Chancellors could point to the resulting trade deficit and justify a credit squeeze to defend our foreign reserves and check inflation. It was the adoption of a floating £ in 1971 that finally removed any external discipline against the faster monetary expansion which propelled our costs and prices upwards faster than in other countries.

Macro-government v. micro-markets

Not only did inflationary 'full employment' policy increasingly lose its intended effect as a stimulant, it acted rather as a sedative that sapped the will to tackle the root causes of the British disease. The macro-economic approach launched by Keynes in 1936 directed attention to the national totals of employment and investment as the chief determinants of output and consumption. It was proof of the Keynesian domination after 1945 that few economists[7] questioned whether

[7] A notable exception was Colin Clark in *Growthmanship*, Hobart Paper 10, IEA, Second Edition, 1962.

the *quantity* of investment was a sufficient guide to policy without concern for its *quality* as determined by the extent to which it was worked efficiently to produce goods and services for sale at home or abroad at competitive prices that yielded a profit above their costs. Successive national plans, from Stafford Cripps's after 1945 to George Brown's in 1965, solemnly listed targets for employment and investment in various industries. But there was no sign of awareness that, in the absence of war-time direction, an improved distribution of re-sources depended on appropriate relationships between market prices, wages and profits. In other words, fashionable obsession with abstract macro-government targets drove out concern for the micro-market reality of individuals as workers, managers and investors whose combined efforts and diverse decisions in response to prevailing incentives must ultimately shape the econ-omic fortunes of a free society.

Practical men, especially 'pragmatic' politicians, do not like being asked to make explicit the theory on which their programmes are necessarily if implicitly based. As a caution to British Social Democrats I suggest the following as a rough formulation of the theory behind most proponents of 'mixed economy'. The unspoken assumption is that with the help of various bureaucratic, academic or business élites, politicians can discern which industries should develop; and the mechanism of enforcement is a mixture of appeals to the 'public interest' reinforced by discretionary tax concessions, contracts, or subsidies. It was this kind of political intervention that explains the long mismanage-ment in steel, ship-building, docks, motor cars, atomic power, coal, railways, development areas.

In contrast, the basic theory underlying market

analysis—glimpsed by some of the ablest young Social Democrats—is that changing opportunities are best indicated by movements in relative prices and profits which supply at once both the information and the incentive for action. Here is the wisdom of a long line of economic thinkers from Smith, Mill, Marshall to Mises, Robbins, Hayek—and even Keynes in his more reflective moods. Indeed, in the concluding notes to *The General Theory* Keynes thought it necessary to remind his readers of the advantages of individualism:

> 'They are partly advantages of efficiency—the advantages of decentralisation and of the play of self-interest. The advantage to efficiency of the decentralisation of decisions and of individual responsibility is even greater, perhaps, than the nineteenth century supposed; and the reaction against the appeal of self-interest may have gone too far. . . .'[8]

Seeds of decline

The late Professor G. C. Allen drew on his unrivalled knowledge of industrial development to chart the beginning of Britain's relative decline from the closing years of the 19th century.[9] Of course, the loss of international leadership in the staples of textiles, steel, ships, coal was inevitable with the rise, in particular, of America and Germany. But he pointed to the unenterprising, protective response of both politicians and fashionable opinion:

> 'The chief effect of the government's intervention between the wars was to defend the failures rather than to encourage the enterprising.'

[8] Keynes, *op. cit.*, p. 380.
[9] In *The British Disease*, Hobart Paper 67, IEA, Second Edition, 1979.

Professor Allen had a good deal to say about the development of ideas unsympathetic or hostile to private enterprise which came to infect politicians and business spokesmen, as well as teachers and civil servants. An even sharper critique of the pervasive indoctrination against the wholesome market ethos was recently presented by an American historian, Professor Martin Wiener, in a slim volume with the striking title *English Culture and the Decline of the Industrial Spirit 1850-1980*.[10] In an impressionistic survey, he offers a wealth of quotations from poets, novelists, artists, academics, philosophers, churchmen, and even successful entrepreneurs turned paternalists, all mocking the prime mover of individual exertion in a competitive economy as 'base materialism', 'money grubbing', 'mere money making', 'philistine', 'sordid', 'shameful'. Institutions as apparently diverse as the Fabian Society, public schools, trade unions, the church, the Tory Party since Disraeli and the Liberal Party since Lloyd-George, to say nothing of the Labour Party since its spawning by the trade unions in 1906, actively or passively contributed to an ethos that spread doubts about the social utility of industry and commerce.

Professor Wiener's explanation is that in Britain the rising bourgeois culture never finally triumphed over the declining aristocratic values, but declared a truce, it might be said, on the playing fields of Eton.[11] The political gains from continuity, stability, and 'peaceful accommodation' were bought at high economic cost to

---

[10] Published by CUP, 1981.

[11] Professor Wiener sums up: 'The educated young men who did go into business took their anti-business values with them'.

the dynamic change necessary for industrial renewal and progress.

Unleashing the vote motive

It should now be easier than in 1936 to see that what Keynes called the 'reaction against the appeal to self-interest' has not only proved costly, but was based on an intellectual error. The burgeoning American literature on the economic analysis of politics has finally exposed the lofty pretension that the unlovely but unavoidable pursuit of self-interest is easily subdued by extending the benign power of government over the market economy. Theory is confirmed by the daily evidence of democratic practice that politics does not supplant what Adam Smith described more objectively as the 'effort of every man to better his condition', which he shrewdly argued was 'the principle from which public and national as well as private opulence is originally derived'.[12]

What we have seen in the rapid post-war extension of government is the diversion of the most naked self-interest through the electoral system into an almost universal scramble for increased benefits of every description. However much the lobbies of business men, trade unionists, tenants, farmers, welfare claimants or multiplying 'minorities' dress up their demands by appealing to 'the national interest', the reality is more often a search for protection, privileges or direct payments at the expense of taxpayers, landlords, investors or consumers. The Hobbesian civil war of 'all against all' has been the direct result of unleashing the vote motive among democratic politicians armed with

[12] *The Wealth of Nations*, ed. Edwin Cannan, Bk. IV, Ch. V, p. 49, Methuen, 1904 (Sixth Edition, 1950).

unlimited governmental discretion to over-rule prices and incomes established objectively between producers and consumers in a competitive market. It explains the instability of the 'mixed economy' and the cumulative extension of government at the expense of the market economy which has brought traditional party loyalties into dispute.[13] Once politicians grant favours to particular sectional interests, other groups of voters have not been slow in pressing their demands and learning from trade unions how to organise, agitate and, if necessary, demonstrate to gain what they want. Thus the senate of contending philosophies has been corrupted into a snake-pit of hostile factions.

Three imperatives for social democracy

There is room here to touch on only three of the most damaging consequences for economic efficiency, which the Social Democrats must find ways of avoiding. The first is that the mounting cost of buying votes raises taxes which blunt incentives to work and increasingly distort effort and investment into politically profitable channels. A radical party should give high priority to reducing taxes. The second is that resistance to paying taxes drives Chancellors into financing higher spending by burdensome borrowing and the implicit tax of inflation. A responsible party should aim to finance tax reductions by cutting public spending. The third, and perhaps most deep-seated ill-effect of governmental weakness in the face of sectional producer interests, is that management and workers seek shelter in politicised subsidies and protection from the economic

[13] In *Britain Against Itself* (Faber, 1982), Professor Samuel Beer points to the new phenomenon after 1970 of MPs voting against their parties even on three-line whips.

imperative of adapting to change by improving their competitive efficiency. It is this weakness of unlimited government since the war that explains the enfeebled rigidity of so much British industry now tardily forced to adapt to the deepest economic recession this century. The degree to which most Western societies are grappling with popular opposition to necessary change indicates the extent of the 'mixed economy' consensus which has led democratic governments to give short-term social-political objectives priority over the pervasive economic prerequisites for mobility, flexibility and incentive. A democratic party should embrace limited government by confining politics to tasks that cannot be discharged by competitive markets.

Limits of government

Outside the blinkered Labour Party there is scope for fruitful discussion about the balance to be struck between government and the market. Well-disposed democrats can differ about the precise boundaries of 'public goods' which can be financed only through the tax system rather than through choice and payment in market prices. Some may prefer governments to set more rigorous standards than others as the framework for the interplay of competitive supply and consumer demand. Above all, judgements may differ about the scale on which the community provides a minimum income for people unable to maintain themselves by their own efforts in the free market. The chief conflict here is between the emotional-aesthetic appeal of equality and the political-economic imperative of incentive for a free and efficient society. The occupational hazard for Social Democrats is that they are tempted by the visible (and electoral) appeal of re-distribution of income and wealth to neglect the damage higher taxes inflict on the hidden processes by which income and wealth are created.[14]

But no candid friend of democracy can deny that, even for the most public of public goods, government provision always and necessarily rests on coercing the minority—if not the majority—to pay more taxes and forego personal preferences. A strong case might be made for proportional representation, but no conceivable reform of the electoral system can make the periodic ballot as responsive to individual choice as the daily referendum of the market. From this simple truism follows the cardinal principle that the more widely even the most truly representative government extends its power over economic and social life, the more difficulty it will have in mobilising consent for its essential purposes, let alone conformity to its multiplying exactions. Whether the 'black economy' accounts for $7\frac{1}{2}$ per cent or nearer 15 per cent of total national income,[15] it is an alarming sign of the spreading rejection of government.

Labour fundamentalists and high Tory paternalists might seek to restore the legitimacy of overgrown government by variants of the corporate state, resting on a concept of 'concertation' with 'representatives' of powerful interests in trade unions and business. The remnants of the once great Liberal Party share the doubts of the new Social Democrats and other radicals

---

[14] One of the most encouraging recent portents was an emphatic speech by David Owen to the Child Poverty Action Group (16 April 1983) urging 'a policy of selectivity and abandoning universality as a welfare principle'.

[15] *Journal of Economic Affairs*, Vol. I, No. 4, July 1981, and Vol. II, No. 3, April 1982.

about such a flirtation with national socialism but fall
back on decentralisation and participation. The approaches of both groups are still flawed in sharing an
essentially élitist approach to the necessary consensus.

When Mrs Shirley Williams entitled her personal
manifesto *Politics is for People*,[16] she unwittingly
revealed the myth shared by socialists of all parties,
namely that most people wish to devote much of their
time to what they regard as the ping-pong of politics.
A truer assertion would be that politics is for political
people, that is, for the minority who care for party
before family and personal life. For the majority, the
more widely their political interest is dissipated, the
more difficulty in focussing it on broad or remote
causes that call for redress by political means. In terms
of active participation and commitment, can there be
serious dispute that it is the ubiquitous market which
best engages the diverse purposes and preferences of
the vast majority of ordinary citizens, especially the
politically maladroit? Sufficient proof is provided by
the pervasive evidence of discontent with one aspect or
another of state schools, hospitals, nationalised industries, council houses, local services, compared with the
remarkable — if generally unremarked — satisfaction
people derive from the post-war transformation of
their owner-occupied homes, modern kitchens, central
heating, double glazing, hi-fi and video equipment,
fashion gear, motor cars, gardens, foreign holidays—
where inarticulate minorities have their say in the
market along with the rest.

It is hardly a matter of ideology to recall the time-
less wisdom of John Stuart Mill:

[16] Penguin Books, 1981.

'. . . the mode in which the government can most surely demonstrate the sincerity with which it intends the greatest good of its subjects, is by doing the things which are made incumbent upon it by the helplessness of the public, in such a manner as shall tend not to increase and perpetuate, but to correct that helplessness . . .

'. . . government aid . . . should be so given as to be as far as possible a course of education for the people in the art of accomplishing great objects by individual energy and voluntary co-operation.'[17]

If the newly emerging political alignment in Britain is to serve the dispersed interests of ordinary people, it should as inconspicuously as possible concentrate on things an increasingly prosperous population cannot do for itself, and for the rest create a framework for competitive markets to serve the most widely-shared interest of diverse individuals as self-reliant consumers. As all the greatest economic liberal philosophers taught, it is the sovereign consumer interest in a competitive market that provides the most enduring basis for a harmonious consensus and that is alone consistent with the advancement of political freedom, moral striving and economic progress.

A challenge to the 'mould breakers'

Even by Western European or Scandinavian standards, Britain approaches 1984 as a highly collectivist economy. Many yet outside the ranks of the Social Democratic Party may welcome its declared aim to 'break the mould' of the post-war consensus which, bereft of secure anchorage in principle, has drifted inevitably

---

[17] J. S. Mill, *Principles of Political Economy*, Longmans, London, 1848, Bk. V, Ch. XI, p. 978.

away from individual freedom towards the all-powerful state.

On the eve of 1984, a new party claiming to re-invigorate democracy could hardly do better than ponder the magisterial words of A. V. Dicey before the outbreak of the First World War:

'The beneficial effect of State intervention . . . is direct, immediate and, so to speak, visible, whilst its evil effects are gradual, and indirect and lie out of sight . . . State help kills self-help.

'Hence the majority of mankind must almost of necessity look with undue favour upon governmental intervention. This natural bias can be counteracted by the existence in a given society, as in England between 1830 and 1860, of a presumption or prejudice in favour of individual liberty. . . .'[18]

The evidence of disarray in all Western democracies confirms the classical economic analysis that the imbalance between government and market has everywhere come to place excessive burdens not only on politicians and their bureaucracies but on voters as citizens and taxpayers. The challenge for a party claiming to 'break the mould' is to indicate how and where it would cut back the over-extended activities of central and local government in Britain, as well as the mounting restrictions and regulations from their beloved Brussels. Politicians who will not discard their excess baggage cannot claim to lead the climb back to the higher ground of freedom where alone lasting prosperity will be found.

[18] A. V. Dicey, *Law and Opinion in England*, Macmillan, 1914, pp. 257-8.

THREE

INFLATION AND THE LABOUR MARKET

Geoffrey E. Wood

*Centre for Banking and International Finance,
The City University*

The Author

GEOFFREY E. WOOD: Born 1945, educated at Aberdeen Grammar School, University of Aberdeen (MA, First Class Honours in Economics, 1967) and University of Essex (MA in Economics, 1968). Lecturer in Economics, University of Warwick, 1968-75; Senior Lecturer in Banking and International Finance, City University, 1976-82; Reader since 1982. Visiting Scholar, Federal Reserve Bank of St. Louis, 1977-78. For the IEA he wrote (with Gordon Pepper) *Too Much Money . . .?* (Hobart Paper 68, 1976) and 'The Purposes of British Taxes', in *The State of Taxation* (IEA Readings 16, 1977), and he contributed an essay, 'Should the Government Change Course in 1982', to its symposium, *Could Do Better* (IEA Occasional Paper 'Special', No. 62, 1982). He has contributed articles to *Southern Economic Journal, Journal of International Economics, Scottish Journal of Political Economy, European Economic Review,* and *American Economic Review.*

Inflation and the Labour Market

Governments have always been involved in the economies of their countries. Sometimes the involvement has taken the form only of buying services and goods by funds raised from taxation, but more often there has been interference, more or less detailed, to promote some desired objective. Protection has been given to individual industries. There have been attempts to influence the distribution of income or wealth. Efforts have been made to stabilise prices and, in this century, to influence the level of economic activity. Throughout the 20th century, these efforts have become more ambitious, and more detailed, in their aims. But success has been in almost inverse proportion to ambition. A conscious, pre-announced, intention of doing less will produce better results than the energetic striving which has characterised particularly the years since 1945.

The announcement of an intention to try less hard does not have to depend on the emergence of a new political party. But that is an opportune occasion, as a new party is not burdened by having to admit its past policies as a mistake. A policy of trying less hard so as to achieve more is on this ground alone readily adopted by Social Democrats.

The argument why it should be is developed in three stages. First, how best to stabilise the economy; then, what can be done to stabilise the economy in the best available situation, in particular on prices, economic activity, and prosperity; finally, the implications of these recommendations for the allocation of output and the distribution of income. The arguments are summarised in the conclusion.

1. STABILISATION

(i) *The failure of 'fine tuning'*

UK Governments have, until the present Administration, consistently regarded 'full employment' as an important objective of policy, but without considering whether that is a meaningful concept. They have therefore applied stimuli to monetary demand whenever it has been believed that unemployment was 'too high', i.e. too far from 'full employment'. What has been the record of this policy?

It is useful first to examine the record of the past three 'reflations'. These periods are defined for this purpose as episodes when the Public Sector Borrowing Requirement (PSBR) rose sharply as a share of gross domestic product (GDP) in money terms and was sustained for two years. The episodes also, it should be emphasised, are occasions when there were conscious efforts to raise the PSBR—or at any rate conscious tolerance of this as a by-product of other policies. The data do *not* include periods when the PSBR/GDP ratio rose because GDP fell.

Data summarising these three reflations are set out in Table 1. The three episodes occurred in the years 1966-67, 1973-74, and 1978-79.

The record is clear. 'Reflation' has only occasionally been successful in offsetting the trend rise in unemploy-

TABLE 1

THE LAST THREE REFLATIONS

		Unemployment	Inflation	Interest Rates**
		%	%	%
1966-67	Before*	1·4	4·4	6·3
	During	1·9	2·4	6·9
	After*	2·4	5·1	8·3
1973-74	Before	3·6	8·2	8·9
	During	2·3	16·0	12·8
	After	4·6	20·3	14·4
1978-79	Before	5·5	12·0	13·6
	During	5·5	13·4	12·7
	After	8·7	15·0	15·9

Source: 'Alternatives to Thatcherism', Commentary in *Annual Monetary Review*, No. 3, Centre for Banking and International Finance, The City University, London, December 1981.

Notes: *'Before' refers to the average of the two years preceding the reflation and 'after' to the average of the subsequent two years.

**Interest rate is the yield on long-dated gilts.

ment, and then only temporarily. Further, those temporary successes have led to higher inflation and higher interest rates. These policies can certainly not be described as successful.

This record of failure is not a recent one. Indeed, it simply up-dates an existing record. In his classic study, *The Management of the British Economy 1945-1960*,[1] Mr J. C. R. Dow concluded that 'stabilisation' policy in the UK had in practice made fluctuations in econ-

[1] CUP for the NIESR, 1964.

TABLE 2

THE LAST THREE INCOMES POLICIES

Policy		Growth of Money Wages (% p.a.)		
		Before	During	After
1972-73	Freeze	21	3	19
1975-76	£6 Flat	33	4	19
1978-79	5% Nom.	19	12	20

Source: 'Alternatives to Thatcherism', op. cit.

omic policy larger than they would have been without attempts to stabilise it. This finding was duplicated by Bent Hansen, for a later period and for a wider range of conditions, in his *Fiscal Policy in Seven OECD Countries 1955-65.*[2]

It is clear that attempts to manage demand have not been successful. Why?

(ii) *Explanations of failure*

The explanations of this record of failure are in three categories. First, there is that of a very small but very vocal group, of which Lord Kaldor is a prominent member. His views are set out with characteristic clarity and vigour in his recently published *The Scourge of Monetarism.*[3] Insofar as stabilisation policy goes, governments did not go far enough, were too concerned with the monetary consequences of their fiscal policies—consequences which, Kaldor implies, should be viewed as trivial by-products—and did not make sufficient use of incomes policies.

What effects have incomes policies had in the UK? It is helpful to look at the last three policies. They are summarised in Table 2.

[2] OECD, Paris, 1969.   [3] Oxford University Press, 1982.

What these three episodes have in common is that they roughly worked when the policy was on, but were followed by a surge of money wages. This characteristic they share with previous policies. The policy affected only the time-profile of the growth of money wages.

Some have argued that the appropriate response to this manifest failure is to keep the policy on for ever. A most complex scheme has been set out by Professor J. E. Meade,[4] and also by Professor Richard Layard.[5] The scheme would tax wage increases above a certain limit. It would thus inhibit relative price movements. As will be argued below, this is a major defect. There are also several other objections to this scheme; they are discussed in the *Annual Monetary Review* (No. 3).[6] It would be going too far afield to consider these policies further; here it is sufficient to note that UK incomes policies have been breaking down before they have been abandoned. A policy has never been abandoned in the full flower of success. Hence proponents of a permanent incomes policy must have as part of their design an explanation of how their policy is to avoid this problem. None has yet faced this issue.

In opposition to the view that policy has been insufficiently vigorous is the argument that, although correct in principle, it was *too* vigorously applied. Governments tried to 'fine tune' the economy to a degree of precision not possible given the knowledge we possess of such

[4] J. E. Meade, *Wage-Fixing*, Allen & Unwin, 1982.

[5] R. Layard, 'Is Incomes Policy the Answer to Unemployment?', Inaugural Lecture presented at the LSE on 7 October 1981, LSE Centre for Labour Economics, Discussion Paper No. 99, October 1981.

[6] 'An Improved Formula for Incomes Policy', *Annual Monetary Review*, No. 3, pp. 9-16, Centre for Banking and International Finance, The City University, London, December 1981.

important factors as time-lags. Had we been a little less ambitious, de-stabilisation would have been avoided. This acknowledges that the kind of failure anticipated in Milton Friedman's 1946 response to the passing of the US Employment Act has occurred, but it still considers that a policy of demand management is possible in principle.

Such a position is, at first glance, hard to refute. It is modest, and has an infinite number of fall-back positions. But there is a fundamental criticism of it. Although many economists are associated with this criticism, its leading proponent is undoubtedly Professor Robert E. Lucas, who has provided a very clear statement of his views in 'Rules, Discretion, and the Rôle of the Economic Adviser',[7] so a brief summary here will suffice.

Lucas pointed out (not a new idea, but one of whose full implications he was the first to make us aware) that behaviour is influenced by expectations of the future. Unless one knows people's expectations, their behaviour cannot be anticipated. The likely future course of economic policy is an important influence on expectations. Unless policy is conducted by rules, we cannot know expected future policy. Hence conducting policy by rules serves two purposes. First, it contributes to the stability and prosperity of the economy by reducing some of the uncertainty inevitably attaching to the future. Secondly, discretionary policy is avoided—and discretionary policy is *inevitably* uncertain in its effects.

It is this last point that is so damaging to the case for demand management; for it emphasises that, if expectations matter at all for economic decisions (and

[7] In *Studies in Business-Cycle Theory*, Basil Blackwell, Oxford, 1981.

the evidence is overwhelming), demand management—
that is, the use of *discretionary* policy to achieve
desired behaviour from the economy—is impossible in
principle.[8]

(iii) *Social Democrats and stabilisation policy*

The first recommendation for Social Democrats, then,
is that the instruments of economic policy should be
operated according to a set of *pre-announced* rules—for
taxation, borrowing, spending and money growth.
There may at first glance appear nothing particularly
'social democratic' about that—and, indeed, there need
not be. The recommendation can simply be on the pragmatic grounds that, for social democrats, adopting it
need not be preceded by admission of past errors. It
has, however, been forcefully argued by Professor F. A.
Hayek that government by rules is essential to the
preservation of any state which cherishes individual
liberty.[9] Hence Social Democrats have a very strong
political motive for adopting such a policy, apart from
the economic imperative that it is the only workable
policy.[10]

---

[8] Those who argue that the years of most active demand management were years of rapid growth should consider R. C. O.
Matthews, 'Why has Britain had Full Employment Since the
War?', *Economic Journal*, September 1968. Professor Matthews
there demonstrates that growth did not result from policies.

[9] *Law, Legislation and Liberty*, 3 Vols., 1973-79, especially
Vol. 3: *The Political Order of a Free Society*, Routledge and
Kegan Paul, London, 1979.

[10] Details of the rules need not be set out here. Discussion can
be found in 'Should the Government Change Course?', in
Could Do Better, Institute of Economic Affairs Occasional
Paper No. 62, March 1982. Note also that the rules need not
[*Contd. on p. 42*]

2. INFLATION

How would that policy lead to the control of inflation? For simplicity, assume that when the Social Democrats take office, inflation is at an acceptable rate—which should be a trend of surely no more than 1-2 per cent. Figures like 5 per cent may now seem attractive, but the deceptions of such attraction may be observed when it is recollected that, even at that modest rate, money halves in value every 14 years. Monetary policy should take the form of a steady rate of growth of the money supply. This should be at a pre-announced rate, and the rate should be no higher than the real-terms rate of growth of the economy, so as to ensure long-run price stability.

At this point, some technicality is necessary so as to cover two questions: first, which money supply?, and, second, over what period should money growth be stabilised?

For money supply, what should be controlled is the stock of reserve assets available to the banking system —the monetary base. That constrains *all* the monetary aggregates, and over a period of 2-3 years these have in the past moved together. Setting such a policy rule in place thus makes certain problems disappear; for it is only if the pre-occupation is with short-term policy that the choice between aggregates is pressing.

Over what period should the money supply be controlled? Should the monetary authority correct devi-

[*Contd. from p. 41*]
be for *constant* behaviour of these policy instruments. The rules can be *contingent*—that is, the instruments respond in a *pre-announced way* to the behaviour of the economy. (E.g., W. H. Buiter, 'Some Unpleasant Monetarist Arithmetic', in *Monetarism in the UK*, Macmillan Press (forthcoming).)

ations from the target rate of growth of money after a month, a quarter, or what? This question is really unanswerable. It turns upon how quickly the economy responds to monetary fluctuations.

It has been well known for many years that, if these fluctuations are believed to be temporary, they will have little effect. No-one will change prices or output. Essentially, then, what matters is the central bank's record. The more trustworthy the central bank is in sticking to its targets, the less will people worry about deviations from them, because these will be perceived as temporary.

I have taken for granted that control of the money supply will control inflation. No mention is made of incomes policies, because of the evidence of their failure, together with their manifest lack of desirability. Nor is any mention made of interest rates. The reason for this is straightforward. Under an interest-rate rule the public correctly anticipates that the authorities will supply whatever nominal money stock is required to maintain the rate of interest. Hence an external shock to the price level, such as the 1973-74 oil price rise, will be matched by a monetary adjustment. The price level is in meta-stable equilibrium, settling down wherever random shocks take it. The future price level cannot be anticipated. This is *not* a consequence of choosing the wrong interest-rate rule. It is an inevitable consequence of choosing any interest rate as a target.

There is nothing specifically 'social democratic' about this approach to inflation—it is simply an aspect of the revolution in economic policy which the lack of historical baggage may permit. Nor, certainly, will this policy control the price level perfectly. The price level in the short run is affected by many factors as well as money growth. What it *will* do is to control the *trend* of prices.

That is all governments can deliver, and all they should promise.

3. UNEMPLOYMENT AND THE LABOUR MARKET

(i) *Wages and prices*

So far the policies advocated as compatible with social democracy are an extension of those of the present Conservative administration. Rules are to cover a wider range of policy instruments, and be announced over a longer period. There is a break in kind with every post-war government except the present one—but only a difference in degree from it.

In their attitudes to unemployment and the labour market, Social Democrats should be much more radical. They should remember that the labour market is a market for labour, and that wages are simply prices—like any other price.

What people are paid should be separate from any notion of 'fairness' or equity. Failure to divorce the two makes the economy worse off, and, whatever benefits it brings to some groups, makes other groups worse off.

(ii) *Wages to allocate resources, not measure 'worth'*

It is becoming commonplace to argue that people should receive a 'fair wage', or a 'living wage', and to claim that, if X per cent can be paid to one group of workers, it can also be paid to another group. The consequences of these arguments can be clearly seen if they are applied to something other than labour. What is a 'fair price' for a pound of apples? If the price of lemons rises by 10 per cent, when on earth is that an argument for the price of turnips rising by the same amount?

These prices move to reflect supply and demand. One price rises relatively to others to reflect relative scarcity; if it were not allowed to do so, the scarcity could not be alleviated, as resources would not be drawn into the activity.

If wages are not allowed to move like every other price, shortages of some jobs and surpluses of others will develop. The economy will be worse off than it should be. There will be no incentives to move geographically or occupationally. The skill structure of the workforce will become ossified.

(iii) *Wages and the excluded worker*

Does that mean we should also abandon minimum wage laws? Unequivocally 'yes'. These laws protect the workers who keep their jobs—and do so at the expense of those who become unemployed, or fail to get jobs because minimum wages are too high. Minimum wages seem charitable—but they are largely charity at the expense of the poor.

(iv) *'Distributive justice'*

This argument does not necessarily imply that we should leave as it is whatever income distribution is produced by the workings of markets. First, we should make the markets as free as possible, removing all artificial barriers to entry—unnecessarily long apprenticeships or professional training, for example. Then, if we are still unhappy about income distribution, we should tax. People do *not* necessarily deserve a living *wage*—what they deserve is a living *income*. Trying to give it through wages is wasteful, and penalises workers who are priced out of work in consequence.

It is no accident that groups of skilled, or monopolistically protected, workers are willing to strike for higher wages for some lower-paid group, but do not ask for higher *taxes* to raise the income of that group. They would have to bear the cost of the second.

We should, however, be cautious about trying to do too much by way of re-distribution. Evidence is accumulating that what is achieved is not much re-distribution at high administrative cost.

4. THE AGENDA SUMMARISED

The macro-economic agenda proposed for Social Democrats has two components. The first is to conduct policy by a set of pre-announced rules. This is an extension of the present Government's efforts in this direction. Secondly, they should recognise that the labour market is a market, treat wages as prices, and distinguish in policy and in public debate between incomes and wages.

The aims of these proposals are modest, but so is our knowledge of the economy. By trying to do less, Social Democrats can achieve more.

FOUR

TAXATION POLICY

A. R. Prest

London School of Economics

The Author

A. R. PREST was born in 1919. He graduated at Cambridge in 1940; PhD, 1948. He held a Rockefeller Fellowship in the USA in 1948-49 and then taught at Cambridge, where he was a Fellow and Bursar of Christ's College, and University Lecturer in Economics. In 1964 he was appointed Professor of Economics and Public Finance and in 1968 Stanley Jevons Professor of Political Economy at the University of Manchester. Since 1970 he has been Professor of Economics (with special reference to the Public Sector) at the London School of Economics. He is a member of the IEA Advisory Council.

Professor Prest is the author of many books mainly in the area of taxation/public finance: *Public Finance in Theory and Practice* (1960); *Public Finance in Underdeveloped Countries* (1962); *Intergovernmental Financial Relations in the UK* (1978); *The Taxation of Urban Land* (1981); (ed.) *The UK Economy* (1966); (ed.) *Public Sector Economics* (1968); (co-author) *Self-Assessment for Income Tax* (1977). For the IEA he has written *The Future of Purchase Tax* (Hobart Paper 8, 1961; 2nd edition with a Postscript, retitled *Reform for Purchase Tax*, 1963); *Financing University Education* (Occasional Paper 12, 1966); *Social Benefits and Tax Rates* (Research Monograph 22, 1970); *How Much Subsidy?* (Research Monograph 32, 1974); and he contributed a paper, 'What is Wrong with the UK Tax System?', to *The State of Taxation* (IEA Readings 16, 1977).

Taxation Policy

It is quite impossible to discuss all the major taxation policy options in any remotely satisfactory way in such a short essay as the present paper. So, rather than treat a large number of topics very superficially, I shall state my views very briefly in an entirely dogmatic way on a wide range of issues and then develop them on two topics recently under intensive discussion—a special tax on excess factor payments and local taxation reform. I shall have nothing to say about the total amount of taxation to be raised but will confine myself entirely to matters affecting the constituent components of whatever is the total tax bill.

1. INEXCUSABLY DOGMATIC ASSERTIONS

(i) *Income tax (and national insurance contributions)*

By far the most important reform here is to expedite the computerisation of the PAYE system. It is nothing short of scandalous that we lag so far behind other industrialised countries in this respect and anything that can be done to hasten the completion date of the computerisation programme (currently 1988) deserves the highest priority.

Computerisation is the key to many other reforms which would take us out of the stone age, in particular the introduction of a non-cumulative instead of the present cumulative PAYE withholding system and a switch to self-assessment.[1] The way would then be open for a lot of others if thought desirable, for example, some form of negative income tax or tax-credits, more effective taxation of short-term social security payments, local income taxation, and so on.

Although the general level of income tax rates and the starting-point for tax can be criticised from various viewpoints, the degree of progression in earned income is not very steep. Indeed, if employers' national insurance contributions were considered to fall on employees, marginal tax rates on earned income could be characterised as being restricted to a range between 45 and 56 per cent.[2]

What clearly is important is that indexation of allowances and higher-rate starting-points should be regarded as a sacrosanct and not merely an optional feature of the system.

There are arguments for abolishing national insurance contributions and levying higher income taxation

---

[1] N. A. Barr, S. R. James and A. R. Prest, *Self-Assessment for Income Tax*, Heinemann for the Institute for Fiscal Studies, London, 1977.

[2] At the bottom end of the tax range an employee pays 30 per cent income tax and 9·0 per cent national insurance contribution (if not contracted out) and his employer pays 10·45 per cent contribution and 1·0 per cent surcharge. So £50·45 would be payable in tax on an 'income' (including employer's payments) of £111·45, making the marginal rate 45·3 per cent. For an employee in the top income-tax bracket for earned income (60 per cent) and above the national insurance upper limit, the marginal £ of earnings only bears income tax. If one assumes membership of an employer's pension scheme with, say, a contribution rate of 6 per cent, his marginal tax rate would be 60 per cent × 94, i.e. 56·4 per cent.

instead, but I am not persuaded by them.[3] It is a fallacy to think that the relative costs of labour and domestically-produced capital goods are affected by the former type of taxation.[4]

(ii) *Capital gains tax*

I favour the indexation of exemption limits for capital gains and their measurement in real terms, but on the other hand am not convinced that some of the reliefs currently in the system, e.g. on gifts in life or at death, are justified. The justification for the present preference in tax rates on capital gains relative to other forms of income also needs to be re-examined rather closely, given that the principle of indexation has been conceded both for exemption levels and measurement of gains.

(iii) *Corporation tax*

The Corporation Tax Green Paper[5] has set out the various options at length. My provisional judgement would be that the imputation system should be retained but that a more far-reaching system of indexation, especially of gains and losses arising from changes in the real value of net monetary liabilities or assets, is called for. (This reform would also have implications for income tax and capital gains tax.)

(iv) *Broad-based taxation of expenditure*

We have to maintain something like the present structure of VAT so long as we are members of the EEC.

[3] A. R. Prest, 'The Structure and Reform of Direct Taxation', *Economic Journal*, June 1979.

[4] C. S. Shoup, *Public Finance*, Weidenfeld and Nicolson, London, 1969, pp. 412-3.

[5] Cmnd. 8456, January 1982.

There are no strong arguments in favour of raising or lowering VAT rates. Nor can it be said that the advocates of general expenditure taxation in lieu of personal income taxation have swept the board of informed opinion.

(v) *Taxes on capital*

The bite of capital transfer tax (CTT) is much less sharp than it was. Indeed, one commentator[6] has argued that the tax has been virtually abolished: 'CTT has become, as Estate Duty was, a voluntary tax'. Since then there have been further relaxations and the principle of indexation for band starting-points has been conceded. The problem is that a highly effective CTT is not easily made compatible with the measures aimed at the encouragement of small business firms.

I have set out my views on a wealth tax on a previous occasion.[7] Despite the predilection of some politicians of some parties for a tax of this kind, and for that matter the recent example of France, it does not seem to me that the game is remotely worth the candle. The equity arguments are not clear-cut but the economic and administrative consequences are only too clear-cut as Ireland found out in its short-lived experiment from 1975 to 1978. It remains true that none of the 'Western' countries levying a tax of this kind derives any revenue of consequence from it. And, to quote one of the most fervent advocates of this tax:

---

[6] A. Sutherland, 'Capital Transfer Tax: an Obituary', *Fiscal Studies*, November 1981, p. 51.

[7] A. R. Prest, 'The Select Committee on Wealth Tax', *British Tax Review*, No. 1, 1976.

'To be effective a wealth tax or a reformed CTT would require the re-introduction of exchange control'.[8]

(vi) *Other taxes*

The substantial excises on mild vices have long been and will long continue to be an essential part of the tax structure even if EEC requirements dictate changes in rate structures. On the other hand, the rationale of stamp duties is extremely weak; and there is really no argument for the special taxation of development gains on land,[9] especially when the tax on land implicit in the absence of any depreciation allowance for commercial buildings and most privately-owned and -rented accommodation is taken into account.

2. A SPECIAL TAX ON EXCESS FACTOR PAYMENTS

The nature of the tax

This is an idea which has received a good deal of publicity in recent months[10] and which has reputedly been received with much sympathy by Mr Roy Jenkins.

[8] TUC Economic Review 1982, *Programme for Recovery*, p. 38.

[9] A. R. Prest, *The Taxation of Urban Land*, Manchester University Press, Manchester, 1981.

[10] It is discussed in the Inaugural Lecture delivered by Professor Richard Layard at the London School of Economics on 7 October 1981, and the article by the same author in *The Guardian*, 13 October 1981. (A revised version of the Lecture is in 'Is Incomes Policy the Answer to Unemployment?', *Economica*, August 1982.) It is also examined in his 'Incomes Policy, Employment Measures and Economic Performance', in *Could Do Better*, IEA Occasional Paper Special, No. 62, 1982. Another source is R. Jackman and R. Layard, 'An Inflation Tax', and R. C. O. Matthews, 'Comment', in *Fiscal Studies*, March 1982.

I shall describe the general nature of the proposals in very broad outline and then examine some of the problems arising, dividing them into a 'Treasury' group and an 'Inland Revenue' group, the former being more economic in character and the latter more operational.

The intention behind proposals of this kind is to help resolve the problem which has dogged the UK economy for years—that one dare not try to raise the level of employment for fear of the effects on the rate of inflation. To this end, it is suggested that a special tax be imposed on employers (*not* employees) related to the difference between earnings levels of the workforce in one period and another. More precisely, a norm would be set for the permitted increase between two periods and the tax on a firm would be based on the difference between the actual and the permitted increase.

In more detail, the difference between payrolls in the two periods would have to be corrected to allow for changes in numbers of employees and in hours worked —since the true quarry is excess increases in earnings per man-hour. It is usually suggested that the tax rate would be substantial, at any rate in nominal terms, so that, say, a 1 per cent transgression above the permitted increase in the (adjusted) wage bill would be accompanied by a tax bill of an equal absolute amount (implying a tax *rate* of 100 per cent). The base period would be continuously rolled forward so that, for instance, the tax bill for the first quarter of 1982 would relate to the difference between the (adjusted) wage bill in that quarter and the wage bill paid in the first quarter of 1981; one would compare the second quarter of 1982 with the second quarter of 1981, and so on.

Another important feature of the proposals is that of budgetary neutrality. The tax would be expressly designed *not* to raise any net revenue: there would be a system of refunds to pay back revenue derived from miscreants to the business sector generally.

Finally, the danger of such a scheme being wrecked by everyone rushing to pay higher wages during the period before the legislation took effect (and thus establishing a higher base so as to minimise future special tax payments) would be minimised by imposing an old-fashioned type of incomes policy clampdown for a year or so.

Questions and difficulties

Such are the bare bones of these highly sophisticated proposals. Fleshing them out raises a host of questions on which there are differing views; I will list some of the more important issues.

1. *The repayment of tax collected:* There are two different points here. One is that, to preserve equity between different firms, those increasing earnings by less than the norm should pay a negative tax. Otherwise, over a period of years one firm which increased wages exactly in line with the norm every year would pay no penalty, yet another firm with the same *average* rate of increase but one which fluctuated more would pay some tax. The second ingredient in the refund mechanism is that any excess of positive over negative tax payments would be distributed to businesses generally, though with some argument about whether it should be on the basis of, say, payroll or numbers employed.

2. *The norm:* Various questions arise such as whether any figure other than '0 per cent' is necessary, which in turn depends on whether the publication

of a higher and perhaps more realistic figure will in itself produce a lower level of wages settlements than otherwise. Another question is how frequently the government should revise the norm.

3. *Coverage:* Private sector coverage might be restricted to firms employing, say, at least 100 workers, each earning more than the minimum level for national insurance purposes. The system would also apply to local government and public enterprises.

4. *The tax base:* Opinion is not unanimous on whether this should be continuously rolled forward or whether there should be a fixed base for a period of years and all excess payments measured from that fixed base.

5. *The tax rate:* The rate might be progressive with, rather than proportional to, payments in excess of the permitted increase.

6. *Dividends:* A system might be envisaged whereby increases in dividend payments as well as wages were also subject to a special 'excess' tax.

(a) *'Treasury' views*

We now come to the main problems facing the Treasury with any scheme of this kind.

First, it is no good introducing such a scheme unless one is confident that it would be effective in stiffening employer resistance to excessive wage demands. There are at least two different sorts of complication here. One is that the potential deterrent effect of any given nominal rate of tax will depend very considerably on whether a firm is liable to step out of line by paying a more than permitted increase one year compensated by a less than permitted increase the following year; or whether excess increases are liable to take place for a number of consecutive years. In the first example, the potential deterrent effect on a wage increase is slight since there will be a negative tax the following year to offset against the positive tax the previous year; but in the second example it may be considerable.

The other complication is that, if the special tax is deductible against corporation tax/income tax—and for various reasons it is hard to envisage it not being so— the effective as distinct from the nominal penalty rate for a firm will depend on the rate of tax it is currently paying on its profits.

Economic effects

A number of economic effects might be expected if the tax did bite. One is that fast-growing firms (or regions) which needed to raise wage levels to attract more labour would be hit harder than others. So would firms making special payments to 'buy out' restrictive labour practices. Strikes consequential on the stiffening of employer resistance to wage increases might also be expected in the initial stages of the policy. Attempts to minimise the impact of the tax by substituting unskilled for skilled labour and thereby reducing the rate of increase in the (adjusted) earnings bill might be acceptable in the short-run situation where the incidence of unemployment is worse for the unskilled, but is not a development to be welcomed over the longer run—and this type of special tax is intended, after all, to be permanent.

Various problems might arise in the public sector. Permitting earnings levels in the central government sector to rise in line with the private sector is not necessarily an appropriate policy, because in some circumstances it might be thought necessary to *increase* the size of the central government sector and that would be likely to require a rate of wage increase faster than in the private sector. There seem to have been some changes of mind on whether the tax would apply to local authorities or not, and the application of the policy to public corporations would obviously be limited if central government subsidies to, say, the National Coal Board were increased to help pay the special tax.

Thought would have to be given to the distributional impact of the tax since, even though it is revenue-neutral, there is no presumption that the joint effects of the tax and the refunds on factor incomes after tax and the prices of goods and services bought would be distributionally neutral as between richer and poorer people.

Finally, the Treasury might take a very jaundiced view of any attempt to apply a similar sort of special tax to dividends.[11] The older inhabitants of Great George Street would shudder at the recollection of wartime excess profits taxation, and *all* the inhabitants, young and old, would remember the complications of limiting dividend increases during the incomes policies of the 1970s. Differential effects on faster-growing firms and incentives to retain a higher proportion of profits would be only two of the undesirable consequences of any such adjustment in policy. Thus, if the political price of introducing a special tax on excess wage increases is a similar sort of tax on excess dividend

---

[11] Cf. Jackman and Layard, *op. cit.*, p. 53: 'To make the tax acceptable it would clearly have to be accompanied by an equivalent control on capital income'.

increases, the case for the former is appreciably weakened.

(b) *'Inland Revenue' views*

What might the Inland Revenue write in briefs advising a Chancellor on these matters?

A first question might well be: Who would pay the tax, and how? There is no case for applying it only to companies and public corporations and omitting unincorporated businesses.[12] Some new special quarterly tax-collection machinery would have to be devised since the payment of such a tax would not fit squarely into any of the existing mechanisms. Exclusion of firms with, say, less than 100 workers would, on the one hand, simplify tax collection very considerably but, on the other, might generate some awkward new problems. Firms might hive off into small non-taxable units those activities particularly prone to excess wage increases; and what would be done about a firm which oscillated in numbers above and below the cut-off point from quarter to quarter?

Earnings data requirements

Earnings data would be the foundation of the tax assessment. But the data currently used for PAYE withholding purposes would not be very satisfactory for the purposes of the new tax. Effective earnings might increase from one year to the next by virtue of increased employer superannuation contributions, but these would not be reflected in the usual data. On the other hand, the Inland Revenue would presumably

[12] Jackman and Layard, *op. cit.*, p. 55: 'In the private sector, it should be confined to companies employing over 100 workers'.

wish to exclude company pension out-payments and so would have to adjust PAYE data accordingly.

After re-defining earnings bills appropriately, it would still be necessary to correct for changes in hours worked and numbers employed. The first of these might be particularly difficult since even data on hours paid for, let alone hours worked, are by no means wholly satisfactory for purposes of this kind. And the following kind of conundrum arises in counting numbers of employees. Firms A and B both raise average hourly earnings of all employees by the same percentage figure; A keeps exactly the same labour force but B substitutes lower-paid female for male labour. Consequently, A's earnings measure goes up by more than that of B, and so A is liable to pay more tax than B.

Scrutinising avoidance devices

Any Inland Revenue official who did not closely scrutinise avoidance devices would obviously be for the chop. The Honourable Society of Lincoln's Inn would have a field day with this tax, as the following illustrations show:

(1) Fringe benefits not officially recorded, or not fully recorded, as earnings.

(2) Self-employment would be substituted for employment.

(3) The ABC firm of the first quarter of 1982 would appear as the XYZ firm of the first quarter of 1983; distinguishing between the genuine new firm not within the tax net and the spurious one trying to escape it might be very difficult.

(4) Mergers and de-mergers might raise many more problems of linking wage bills from quarter to quarter than the advocates of the tax have been prepared to allow.

Not all of these devices are wholly undesirable in themselves; and there are obvious limits to which they could be used. Nevertheless, they could hardly be disregarded.

Finally, the not-so-mythical Inland Revenue official would obviously have to scrutinise not only his own departmental collection costs but also the compliance costs imposed on taxpayers, keeping a watchful eye open for the predictable outcries from the vociferous ranks of businessmen's organisations.

A complex issue—let others experiment first!

How can the economic effects of such a tax be summarised? The outstanding importance of the issue to which these proposals are addressed cannot be denied, nor the failure to solve them so far by other measures. And some of the standard difficulties of taxing differences between two magnitudes do not arise in this case, e.g. the expectation that the tax might be abolished would be conducive to *lower* rather than *higher* increases in wage payments so as to minimise tax bills. But it must be accepted that a tax on these lines is not a simple one to comprehend or to enforce. It was for these reasons that it did not gain much support in earlier discussion.[13]

---

[13] For instance, S. Weintraub, 'An Incomes Policy to Stop Inflation', *Lloyds Bank Review*, January 1971; and L. L. Dildine and E. Sunley, 'Administrative Problems of Tax-Based Incomes Policies', *Brookings Papers*, 1978, No. 2.

So all in all, despite the undeniably attractive features of the proposal, it might be wiser to remember the early history of passenger jet airliners. Let some other country try the experiment first and find out whether there are any disastrous results before embarking on such a policy ourselves.

3. LOCAL TAXATION

A topic on which every government says a lot but does little is local finance. Official documents since 1971 have included Green Papers in 1971, 1977 and 1981, not to mention the Layfield Committee Report and its 10 volumes of Appendices in 1976.[14] These are only the latest in a long line of official publications stretching back to the great inquiries during the early part of the century.[15] There has also been a spate of discussion and comment from private sources over many years.[16] Given the background it seems safe to say that the technical arguments are all known; it is a matter of political willingness to take long-overdue action.

[14] *The Future Shape of Local Government Finance*, Cmnd. 4741, 1971; *Local Government Finance*, Report of the Layfield Committee of Enquiry, Cmnd. 6433 (and Appendices), 1976; *Local Government Finance*, Cmnd. 6813, 1977; *Alternatives to Domestic Rates*, Cmnd. 8449, 1981 (all HMSO, London).

[15] *Royal Commission on Local Taxation, Final Report*, England and Wales: Cd. 638, 1901; *Final Report of the Departmental Committee on Local Taxation*, Cd. 7315 and Cd. 7316, 1914 (both HMSO, London).

[16] To give only two examples, A. R. Prest, *Intergovernmental Financial Relations in the U.K.*, Research Monograph No. 23, Centre for Research in Federal Financial Relations, Australian National University, Canberra, 1978; and C. D. Foster, R. A. Jackman and M. Perlman, *Local Government Finance in a Unitary State*, Allen & Unwin, London, 1980.

Background: decline of local independence

The Layfield Committee pinpointed the basic issue by positing the alternatives of a centralist or a localist solution, depending on whether one is or is not prepared to accept, or indeed expedite, the continuing decline in local authority independence. My own view is that the localist solution is infinitely preferable but restrictions of space prevent me from developing the reasons for such *obiter dicta*.[17] But one objection to the localist solution is so common as to require specific mention: effective demand management necessitates central control of local authority expenditure met from local authority revenue. Some, though not much, support can be given to this idea on familiar balanced-budget multiplier grounds; but that in turn relates to a Keynesian framework of thought and not to the monetarist stance of the present Government.

The basic logic of the localist approach is that, whatever the precise range of local authority functions, dependence on central government grants must be reduced. The precise measurement of such dependence can be debated, but the general picture is that, on any definition, local authorities rely on central government for more than half of their revenue. It is therefore necessary to consider various alternative sources of revenue.

Alternative sources of revenue

These alternative sources—domestic rates, non-domes-

[17] I shall also refrain from comment on the financial implications of proposals for large-scale re-organisations of local authorities or the introduction of regional assemblies such as recently proposed by the SDP in its Green Paper No. 3, *Decentralising Government*, London, July 1982.

tic rates, local income taxation, other local revenue sources, and central government grants—will be considered in turn.

(i) Domestic rates

Domestic rates are paid by some 20 million people each year in Britain and amount to about one-fifth of local revenue. They are a very old-established tax with direct links to the Poor Law Act of 1601 and indirect links to older taxes. They also have many advantages, such as a stable and predictable yield, readiness of attribution to a given local authority area, ease of collection, voluminous case law, and so on. Moreover, domestic property taxation in one form or another is a common source of local finance in other countries; and those few countries which have abandoned it (e.g. Ireland in 1978) have not found the going very easy in its absence. Nevertheless, such taxes have many enemies both on theoretical and practical grounds.

On theoretical grounds, the first objection is that taxation of buildings, as distinct from land, is likely to have disadvantages for resource allocation. This can happen; but in the UK to-day there are very large concessions made to building in other tax contexts— owner-occupied homes and non-liability to income tax and (often) capital gains tax; zero-rating of new construction for VAT; and so on.

A second theoretical argument is that domestic rates are unfair, inequitable and so on. Any such charge has to be substantiated and must depend crucially on how such taxes filter through into goods and factor prices affecting particular income groups. Moreover, even if it were the case that rates were unquestionably harsh on poorer members of the community, the argument does not take us very far since any such effects may easily be offset by those of various other types of government revenues and expenditures. Nor can it be said that domestic rates impinge on only a small number of people. Even though some of those who nominally pay rates recoup such payments from, e.g., supplementary benefit, others bear part of the effective even if not the nominal burden (e.g. lodgers in a rate-paying household).

There are many criticisms of rating practices. These seem to me to be much better founded. It is farcical to stick to a rental basis when there is so little evidence on free-market rents; and it is a scandal that seven years have now passed since the Layfield proposals for capital value rating without any effective action being taken. It is also a disgrace that the system of regular re-valuations has fallen into desuetude. Five-yearly full-scale revaluation, together with more rough-and-ready updating by a price-index in intervening years, would cause far less trouble than re-valuations at very long intervals. Nor would the old canard about lack of buoyancy of rates have any support in such circumstances. Finally, one can only marvel at the ability of the Ministry of (for?) Agriculture to keep the re-rating of agricultural land at bay, not merely year after year but decade after decade.

I would therefore conclude that there is a good deal to be said for domestic rating *provided* the valuation procedure is properly carried out and the distributional consequences are circumscribed.

(ii) *Non-domestic rates*

These amount to about one-quarter of local authority revenues; like their domestic counterpart they are old-established and have many well-tried virtues as a source of local finance. But they are criticised on several grounds. One is that business firms do not benefit directly in the same way as individuals from expenditure on education, by far the biggest item of local authority spending. Another is that there is no business vote in local elections.

These arguments can be overdone. Income tax (or corporation tax) has always applied to the profits of business organisations despite their lack of votes in national elections. It must also be remembered that business rates are a tax-deductible expense. On the other hand, it is true that a local authority can impose a rate on a business firm which in no way falls on the inhabitants of that area. So this does lead to a more careless attitude towards the effects of non-domestic than domestic rating.

There is no perfect solution to these problems. Perhaps the best one is to continue non-domestic rating but to limit very strictly the differential between domestic and non-domestic rating in any one area and the non-domestic variations between areas.

(iii) *A local income tax*

I am an unregenerate supporter of a local income tax. There are, of course, difficulties of principle such as accountability by place of work or place of residence and, if one decides on the latter, which residence of an individual who has two or more homes. But these difficulties have been overcome in other countries and it is ludicrous to argue that solutions cannot be found in Britain. The real difficulty is that we are in a position with our income tax administration similar to that prevailing on the political front before the Reform Act of 1832. It must be accepted that a workable system of local income tax cannot be introduced until the computerisation of PAYE is completed. But having said that one should, as mentioned earlier,

(a) see whether such computerisation really has to take until 1988;

(b) prepare for a switch to non-cumulative withholding and self-assessment as soon as possible after that date; and

(c) fit a local income tax into the system.

The preceding paragraph is a very bald statement of what is required. But this topic has been written about on many occasions and it is quite unnecessary to go into it all again. The balance of advantage seems to me to be decisively in favour of a movement in this direction as soon as possible.

(iv) *Other sources*

Numerous alternative sources of local revenue have been discussed times without number—local sales tax, motor vehicle duties, payroll or employment taxes, assigned revenues and the like. But they have also been rejected times without number and so I do not propose to disinter their corpses here. There is more mileage to be gained from an examination of the scope for charging for more local authority services, but even here it would be unwise to exaggerate the possibilities.[18]

---

[18] A. R. Prest, 'On Charging for Local Government Services', *Three Banks Review*, March 1982.

(v) *Grants*

On grants, the main point is that, if local income tax revenues were added to the local authority tax base largely as an addition to rates, it would be possible to cut grants and thus reduce local authority dependence on central government grants.[19] The precise format of the grant system would no doubt have to change in that the relative position of different authorities might otherwise change very drastically given the modification of the tax base. This would not be easy to implement, but again the experience of other countries does not suggest it is impossible. As for the argument that some local authorities cannot be trusted to behave suitably with a larger tax base of their own because local elections are such an ineffectual operation—why not have a system in which the size of the grant is positively related to the proportion of the electorate voting?

Reflections

The history of local government finance in this country is a very sorry one of interminable discussion (and of declining quality, if one judges it by the Green Paper of December 1981)[20] and of missed opportunities. It was silly to change local authority boundaries, functions, etc., in the early 1970s in advance of financial re-construction; it was rash on the part of the Conservative Opposition in 1974 to promise to abolish domestic rates; and it was extremely short-sighted of the Con-

---

[19] Recent suggestions that the local authority financial problem should be 'solved' by introducing an additional grant for education fail on these grounds alone, quite apart from any others.

[20] A. R. Prest, 'Greener Still & Greener', *Local Government Studies*, Vol. 8, No. 3, May/June 1982.

servative Government of 1979 to cancel plans for rating re-valuation. But if the drift towards further centralisation of political power in this country is to be halted or reversed, major action on the financial front can no longer be left until the Greek Kalends.

4. CONCLUSION

There are many ways in which a short paper on taxation policy can be written. Whether those of a social democratic disposition approve of the technique adopted here—of a very broad brush on some issues and a more detailed examination of two topics of immediate current interest—the categorical imperative is a sense of humility in these matters. Many of the alternatives in the tax sphere have been known and discussed for many years; if there were any easy answers they would by now have been known to everyone—and perhaps even implemented.

FIVE

SOCIAL POLICY FOR SOCIAL DEMOCRACY

Michael Beenstock

City University Business School

The Author

MICHAEL BEENSTOCK: Born 1946, educated at the London School of Economics (BSc(Econ), 1967; MSc, 1968; PhD, 1976). He was Adviser, HM Treasury, 1970-76, on international monetary and energy problems; World Bank (Washington), 1976-78, on project appraisal and development planning; Senior Research Fellow, London Business School, 1978-81. Since 1981 he has been the Esmée Fairbairn Professor of Finance and Investment, City University Business School, and Director of the City Institute of Finance and Economic Review (CIFER). He is author of *The Foreign Exchanges: Theory Modelling and Policy* (1978); *Health Migration and Development* (1980); *A Neoclassical Analysis of Macroeconomic Policy* (1980); *The World Economy in Transition* (1983). For the IEA he has previously contributed a paper, 'Fallacies in Counter-inflation Policy', to its collection of essays entitled *Could Do Better* (Occasional Paper 'Special', No. 62, 1982).

Social Policy for Social Democracy

1. IDEOLOGY IN SOCIAL POLICY

Social policy in ferment

During the 1970s macro-economic policy underwent a revolution. The Keynesian conventional wisdom was challenged by what turned out to be a successful classical (or monetarist) counter-revolution. Within Whitehall in 1975 (I was there) nobody guessed that within two years the conventional wisdom would yield to the ideas of the counter-revolutionary plotters (I was one of them). At the time it seemed simply impossible to do things in a different way and to escape from what Keynes called habitual modes of thought.

During the 1980s there is every possibility that a parallel counter-revolution will take place; this time in the conduct of social policy. The current rumblings about the failures of the National Health Service, the social security system and indeed the Welfare State as a whole, together with the re-discovery and promotion of classical or market-based social policies, are very reminiscent of the rumblings in the macro-economic arena of 10 years ago. The conventional wisdom of the Welfare State is being challenged by what are in fact the long-established ideas of the classical economists. It may well be that the first stage in the counter-revolution in social policy has already begun. If so, the 1980s will emerge as the battleground in which the supporters of the Welfare State and the classicists fight it out; and if the outcome of the battle that took place in the 1970s is anything to go by, social policy in 1990 will be as radically different from social policy in 1980 as was macro-economic policy in 1980 different from its counterpart in 1970.

Nor does the parallel between these two counter-revolutions stop there. In arguing that 'full employment' policies must be abandoned, the classical counter-revolutionaries of the 1970s were regarded as heartless apostles of the Right and vilified as the enemy of the working classes. A similar pattern of vilification is emerging in the 1980s. The classical counter-revolutionaries who are challenging the ideology of the Welfare State are heartless villains lacking a normal concern for humanity. Their motives are a wicked manifestation of the class system, and even if their arguments appear logically consistent they must be resisted in the interests of common humanity.

This assessment is, of course, a perversion of the truth. The counter-revolutionaries have as much concern for humanity as anybody else. The ends are the same; it is only the means which differ. Therefore the counter-revolution is not about the objectives of social policy but the means for successfully achieving those objectives. In this respect the SDP's Green Paper No. 5[1] is progressive in emphasising the NHS as a *means* rather than an *objective* of policy. It is inevitable and understandable that those with vested interests in the conventional wisdom will do all they can to discredit their challengers. In social policy this is much easier

[1] *Fair Treatment: Social Democracy in the Health and Social Services*, Social Democratic Party, London, 1982.

than in macro-economic policy which tends to be more diffuse in nature. It is for this reason that the present counter-revolution will be more hard-fought than its predecessor of the 1970s and the basic arguments of the plotters will be obscured by the tide of emotionalism that the Welfare State tends to conjure up. Image may therefore in the end matter considerably more than substance. This means that the plotters must establish their humanitarian credentials in the battle for public opinion; to win the technical arguments is clearly not enough. The defenders of the conventional wisdom may lose out on cold logic but in many cases the heart cannot fail to warm to them. In contrast, all too often, the counter-revolutionaries succeed in chilling the soul. But perhaps this is a problem for Saatchi and Saatchi and should not detain us here any longer.

Economics and ideology

In its nature, positive economics is value-free in the same spirit that positive science is value-free. The Theory of Relativity in itself is value-free; it is simply a hypothesis about matter. Its applications, however, raise all sorts of ideological and therefore value-laden questions—as evidenced by the anti-nuclear lobby. Positive economics is simply concerned with the objective phenomenon of how the economy works and how economic agents function. If, for instance, it is objectively true that monetary growth induces inflation in the same sense that gluttony induces fatness, it is no good ruling out the hypothesis on ideological grounds. How the world works is a constraint on the normative or ideological objectives we set ourselves. The economist can offer advice on the best way of achieving these objectives in the light of his understanding of how the world works.

If it is true that the market or classical approach to social policy is more efficient in achieving specific social objectives than the statist (welfare state) approach, it is no good ruling out the classical hypothesis on ideological grounds. Only the objectives are ideological, and on them the economist has nothing special to say. All he can do is to advise how the world works and clarify for the ideologue the economic implications of his objectives and the best way of expediting them. Classical economics or, for that matter, any other kind, is no more or less than a hypothesis of how the world works and in itself is value-free. Classical economics might inadvertently challenge existing non-scientific prejudices and orthodoxies. I would put socialism in this category. But this has happened before in the history of science—Galileo *v.* the churchmen, Darwin *v.* the fundamentalists. Galileo and Darwin were not concerned with ideology but simply with how the world worked. The churchmen and the fundamentalists were, in contrast, concerned solely with ideology regardless of how the world worked.

This confrontation very much parallels the clash between classical economics and socialism. But it would be as perverse to pin ideological labels to the classics as it would be to pin ideological labels to Galileo and Darwin. The classics may be wrong just as Darwin and Galileo might be wrong, but that is a different matter entirely.

This dichotomy between economics and ideology has unfortunately not filtered down to the SDP. Green Paper No. 5 is bedevilled by this confusion and the distinction between ends and means is hopelessly blurred. Thus the classical approach is ruled out as 'Tory dogma'. The classical theory of how the world works may be wrong, but this is not what is being said. Instead, the market approach to health care is dismissed on ideological grounds. At the same time, the SDP sets up its own laudable ideology to eradicate various inequalities in health care and to promote more answerability in the health care industry without realising that the classical economic analysis might have lent itself to promote these ends. It is sad that, after all Mr Roy Jenkins's protestations, the SDP has not broken out of the mould of British politics at all: ideology and economics remain as confused as ever.

Ideology for social policy

Although I have argued that economics is not in itself ideological, this view begs the question of what ideology might be sensible in a social democracy, especially as it pertains to social policy. As an economist I can have no view on the matter; as a member of a social democracy I can express my own personal viewpoint. It seems clear from Green Papers Nos. 4[2] and 5 that the basic ideology of the SDP is egalitarianism. There should be equal access to health care, education, etc. At many instances this view is contradicted but, nevertheless, equality emerges as the basic objective of policy. A closer reading, however, suggests that what concerns the SDP is not equality *per se* but the removal of the inequalities that are experienced by certain groups. For instance, the Black Report on Health Inequality[3] is cited

[2] *Foundations for the Future: An Educational Training Policy*, Social Democratic Party, 1982.

[3] *Inequalities in Health: Report of a Research Working Group*, DHSS, 1980.

in the context of objectives to improve the health of the lower socio-economic groups. Similarly, education policy is to some extent geared to raising the prospects of the poorer groups in society.

Now equality and the removal of such inequalities are not the same thing. Indeed, this distinction has been made by the contemporary social philosopher John Rawls, who argues that the objective of society should be to maximise the prospects of its worst-off members.[4] This 'maximin' ideology is a radical alternative to the 'greatest happiness of the greatest number' ideology bequeathed by Bentham and the Utilitarians. To Rawls a just society is one in which its worst-off members are as well off as they can be. This will not typically imply that the just society is egalitarian. On the contrary, egalitarianism would be *unjust* if its consequence was to reduce the prospects of the worst-off groups. Thus the rich can get richer as long as the prospects of the poor are raised as a consequence or are at least not jeopardised.

The focus of policy is therefore on the worst-off groups in society. A compassionate and caring society is not generally the same as an egalitarian society and all too often the opposite is true. With the exception of those who are primarily interested in fighting class wars, it is most probably true that at least the majority of us have Rawlsian rather than egalitarian ideologies. Mr Jenkins may drink his claret as long as the prospects of the worst-off members of society do not suffer as a consequence. And, who knows, their prospects may even be improved! In this event his drinking would be positively just and it would be unjust to tax claret.

[4] J. Rawls, *A Theory of Justice*, Harvard University Press, Cambridge, Mass., 1971.

I think we are all Rawlsians now, but have not yet fully realised the implications—which are important. We do not, for example, *all* have to enjoy free and/or equal access to health services, education, housing, pensions and social security. If such egalitarianism promoted the prospects of the worst-off groups it would be desirable, but this is unlikely to be generally true. It seems more likely that, by giving the rich the same access rights as the poor, the prospects of the latter are almost bound to diminish rather than increase. Yet this is what the Welfare State is all about. Therefore Rawlsian justice is almost bound to preclude the egalitarianism of the Welfare State. Similarly, it does not imply that the rich must be highly taxed in the name of egalitarianism, since the resultant disincentive effects might harm the prospects of the worst-off groups.

From equality to 'maximin'

We must therefore cease to be 'hung up' on equality and establish instead the 'maximin' ideology. The 'maximin' ideology raises numerous practical questions. Which are the worst-off groups? In what sense are they worst-off? What is the economic model that describes their prospects and their relationship with better-off groups? And so on. In the arena of social policy it may be that the worst-off group is not homogeneous: people with the worst housing may not have the worst health, and so on. The practical problems the Rawlsian approach raises are clearly enormous because they are so different from what we are used to. In the meanwhile, all we can propose is to place them on the agenda for social democracy.

2. ASPECTS OF SOCIAL POLICY

In the light of this discussion I now turn to some specific aspects of social policy and explore how classical economics might be geared to a Rawlsian ideology.

Health and education

From a Rawlsian perspective it is unjust that a person such as myself should enjoy free health services because in all probability this is harming the prospects of the worst-off groups. From a selfish point of view I might prefer the present arrangements, but this is hardly the stuff of social justice. The same applies to education except insofar as for social reasons the law stipulates that I have to educate my children whether I like it or not. Classical economics suggests that the health and education industries can be substantially run like any other industry in private markets. As long as these markets are competitive the 'hidden hand' will ensure that society will obtain the health care and education that it desires. The price mechanism will be more efficient than a centralised bureaucracy, and health insurance (at competitive prices) will provide people with cover against health contingencies. Producer answerability will be sharpened by competition. If hospital beds are in short supply, their price will rise and supply will increase. Consumers will prefer to buy lower-priced generic drugs rather than expensive proprietary drugs, and so on.

But what about the worst-off groups that cannot afford these market-determined prices for health insurance and education? According to the classical approach there are two possible answers. The paternalistic one is to provide them with a subsidy to help them pay. It is paternalistic because the subsidy is geared to specific items of expenditure. This method is efficient because resources are being re-distributed to the target group alone. In the limit, the subsidy could take the form of an outright grant. In contrast, the NHS extends the grant to society as a whole, which inevitably leads to an excessive consumption of resources. As a mechanism for reaching the target group, free health is as inefficient as saturation bombing when the target is not the entire city but only the town hall.

The second remedy is not to single out specific items of expenditure such as health and education but to transfer income to the worst-off groups which they can spend according to their own choice. If they do not choose to spend these resources on health or education, this choice is their prerogative which must be respected. I suspect that, if indeed most of us are Rawlsians, we are in practice paternalistic ones.

A Martian visiting Britain for the first time might ask itself—why not have a National Bread Service (NBS) as well as a National Health Service? Bread is just as 'important' as health. The establishment of a NBS would entail the nationalisation of bread production and the provision of free bread, for only in this way could equal access be guaranteed. There would be endless wrangles over what kind of bread should be produced—sliced, thick, granary, etc.—and also where outlets for different types of bread should be sited. There would be questions in Parliament about why the bread in Runcorn was inferior to the bread in Hampstead, and in the absence of competition it would be surprising if the unit price of bread did not rise. Our Martian might be justified in concluding that, instead of pouring resources into NBS it might be better to place both bread and health in the market sector, leaving it to market forces to determine which kinds of bread should be produced and in which areas.

As for those on low incomes, purchasing power for health should be provided on the same basis as purchasing power for bread through the re-distribution mechanisms of the fiscal system. Health and education are not special cases. They have been arbitrarily singled out and people have grown to think there is no other way. Thus the market provides a better means for reaching out to the target group or groups than the method of saturation bombing that underpins the welfare state.

Housing

The state sector in housing is of course much smaller than the state sector in health and education. The principles are, however, essentially the same. The central ideology behind the state sector in housing is to provide houses for people who can least afford them. Thus once more we see that the ideology is Rawlsian rather than egalitarian; there is a worst-off group that society desires to help. We should therefore ensure that *only* the worst-off group benefits from any public resources, and that housing should be supplied from the most efficient source. In view of relative costs, the efficiency criterion most probably rules out the production of housing by local government, while the concentration on the poor would preclude many who are currently benefiting from local government housing.

Fortunately, the situation is not quite as extreme as in health and education, because only about 30 per cent of housing is supplied by the public sector in contrast to more than 90 per cent in education and health. Moreover, it has recently been established[5] that the provision of public sector housing at sub-economic rents reduces labour mobility. Leaving the housing sector to market forces, therefore, would have the additional benefit of increasing the mobility of labour, which would tend in turn to lower unemployment. The worst-off groups would receive either housing subsidies tied to housing along the paternalistic model or income transfers through the fiscal system.

Social security

Classical economics suggests that prices should reflect marginal costs. In the unemployment benefit system exactly the opposite prevails. There is no relationship at all between the risks of unemployment and national insurance contributions, which are by and large related to income alone. Those who face higher unemployment risks should contribute more towards unemployment insurance than those who face lower risks, on exactly the same basis that motor car insurance and other forms of insurance are priced. By the same token, workers should be able to vary the amount of cover they buy at these competitively-determined prices. There must be many unemployed people who wish they had had more cover and were under-insured. Likewise there are many workers who are over-insured and are cross-subsidising other people in the labour market. The entire unemployment benefit system is an absurd

---

[5] G. Hughes and B. McCormick, 'Do Council Housing Policies reduce Migration between Regions?', *Economic Journal*, December 1981.

mess from an economic standpoint and is in need of radical reform.[6]

My own preference would be for the non-paternalistic Rawlsian ideology; I would scrap all benefits in kind and consolidate them into cash[7] on the grounds that people are, or can quickly learn to become, their own best judges of how their income should be spent, although there must be safeguards for children whom society must protect if their parents refuse to do so. A Negative Income Tax system[8] would be applied so that all households have an income safety net (the height of which must be decided by the electorate) and the poverty trap of penal marginal tax rates at low incomes is removed. Quite appropriately, the SDP have singled out this issue in their Green Paper on Social Security[9] and it is an issue that all political parties should carefully consider.

Pensions

As with unemployment benefit, there is no rational economic basis to present arrangements for state and occupational pension schemes. These schemes depend entirely on demographic factors because current workers and employers pay the pensions that the pensioners currently receive. Thus pensions are simply a transfer payment between workers and pensioners. As the number of pensioners rises with the greying of the popula-

---

[6] Specific proposals are discussed in M. Beenstock and S. Billington, 'Rational Pricing of Unemployment Insurance', City University Business School, mimeo, October 1982.

[7] M. Beenstock, 'Poverty, Taxation and the Welfare State', *National Westminster Bank Review*, August 1980.

[8] As outlined, e.g., in Colin Clark, *Poverty before Politics*, Hobart Paper 73, IEA, 1977.

[9] *Attacking Poverty*, Social Democratic Party, 1982.

tion, non-pensioners are penalised for the larger out-goings on pensions. There is no basis for such arrangements either in 'fairness' or in economics.

Instead, pensions must be the income generated by the past savings of the pensioners themselves. Pensioners in 1983 should not therefore be living at the expense of workers in 1983 but on their own cumulative savings in the past. Each pensioner should therefore be responsible for himself. Likewise each worker in 1983 should be saving for his own retirement. He should not be relying on the support of others when he retires; nor should he be supporting existing pensioners during his working years. If the ratio of pensioners to workers was always constant and the real value of pensions was constant, our present arrangements would be crude but reasonably fair. But neither of these factors is constant over time. On the contrary, both are rising sharply and this is placing a very heavy burden on the present generation of workers, a burden which will bear no relationship at all to the pensions they will receive when they eventually retire.

People should pay the market price for their pension rights. The most effective way of doing this is to leave people to arrange their own pensions in the financial markets, or to employ pension fund managers. They would then be free to choose their optimal age of retirement as they, rather than the state, saw fit. They would also regard that part of their gross income which presently goes to the pensions of others as part of their net income; this change would be likely to improve work incentives.

The practical task of government is to devise the transition from the present muddle to an ordered system, but we must first see clearly where we wish to go.

3. CONCLUSIONS

The classical or market approach to social policy is as compassionate as and more effective in reaching down to deprived groups than our present arrangements. The debate about the Welfare State is solely a technical issue about means; it is not a debate about the goals of social policy. The Welfare State is an inefficient delivery system but people are frightened that its removal would automatically constitute a return to the dark ages. Nothing could be further from the truth. The agenda for social democracy must discuss the compassionate side of the market approach to social policy.

SIX

SOME SUGGESTIONS FOR UK COMPETITION POLICY

S. C. Littlechild

University of Birmingham

The Author

STEPHEN LITTLECHILD: Professor of Commerce, University of Birmingham, since 1975. Formerly Professor of Applied Economics, University of Aston, 1973-75. Sometime Consultant to the Ministry of Transport, Treasury, World Bank, Electricity Council, American Telephone & Telegraph Co., Department of Energy. Author or co-author of *Operational Research for Managers* (1977), *Elements of Telecommunication Economics* (1979), and *Energy Strategies for the UK* (1982). For the IEA he wrote *The Fallacy of the Mixed Economy* (Hobart Paper 80, 1978), and contributed to *The Taming of Government* (IEA Readings 21, 1979). Member of the IEA Advisory Council since 1982. He was commissioned by the Department of Industry to consider proposals to regulate the profitability of British Telecom. His Report, published in February 1983, was substantially accepted by the Government.

Some Suggestions for UK Competition Policy*

1. INTRODUCTION

The SDP's present attitude to competition is set out in its policy document on *Industrial Strategy*.[1] It shows a welcome appreciation of the constructive role which markets and competition can play.

> 'The central aim of SDP industrial policy should be to develop a vigorous private business sector, capable of competing internationally with our overseas rivals. . . .
>
> For the vast majority of business most of the time, it is the proper working of competitive markets which will ensure their efficiency and their contribution to wealth and employment.' (pp. 17-18)

The present Conservative Government (in contrast to its predecessor) has also re-affirmed its faith in competition by such measures as the abolition of exchange control, resistance to import controls and initial steps towards the privatisation of the nationalised industries.

This shift in political attitudes has been matched by an analogous shift in the views of economists. Nowadays, the strength of competition is less often judged

---

*I am grateful to Professors M. E. Beesley, J. F. Pickering and B. S. Yamey, and to Messrs. M. Howe and M. Wright for comments and suggestions on earlier drafts of this paper, though none of them should be held responsible for the final content.

[1] Policy Document No. 2, debated and approved by the Council for Social Democracy on 15 October 1982.

merely by the number of firms in the market at a specific time; more emphasis is attached to conditions of entry and the challenge of new products and techniques. There is increasing recognition that many forms of market conduct previously thought to be monopolistic may be better understood as reflecting an attempt to compete in an environment which is complex and uncertain. There is also a growing acknowledgement that the major restrictions on competition derive not from the actions of firms but from the actions of governments.

In the light of these changing political and economic views, it seems appropriate to re-appraise UK competition policy, which has been steadily expanding in scope over the last 35 years or so. Policy on restrictive practices, anti-competitive practices, mergers and the nationalised industries will be examined. Reference will be made to SDP policy recommendations insofar as these are explicit, but it is hoped that the analysis and suggestions which follow will be of interest to any government wishing to protect and enhance competition.

2. RESTRICTIVE PRACTICES

UK competition policy has remained consistently pragmatic, in the sense that the advantages and disadvantages of any action or agreement may—indeed must—be appraised before coming to a judgement about the public interest. Nevertheless, the verdicts of the Restrictive Practices Court have been such as to establish a general expectation that restrictive agreements will not be approved.

On the whole, this seems a satisfactory outcome. The

potential merits of the agreements (e.g. in protecting firms against excessive uncertainty) have not gone unappreciated, but have generally been outweighed by the expected disadvantages (e.g. of restricted price competition). Firms at least have the significant advantage of knowing where they stand on public policy. One adverse consequence, however, has been the increased incentive not to register agreements or not to comply with adverse Court judgements. Penalties for failure to register or comply need to be increased. Triple damages (as in the US system) might be awarded to those parties adversely affected by non-registration or non-compliance, since such parties have the most ability to discover and prosecute unregistered collusion.

In 1973, restrictive practices legislation was extended to include services. This was an important and welcome development. Travel agents have just defended their agreements, with members of the Stock Exchange following in January 1984. The delay of over seven years since these service agreements were registered stands in marked contrast to the two years required to bring the first agreements to Court after the 1956 Act. This delay, which Mr Justice Lincoln recently described as 'appalling', is apparently due to pressure of work at the Office of Fair Trading (OFT). It would seem desirable for the OFT to transfer more of its limited resources to this area; other activities which might usefully be cut back will be identified later.

Action to curb professional restrictions

Action on the professions is long overdue. The restrictions on advertising enforced by the main professions have already been critically reviewed, and a few modi-

fications have belatedly ensued. The Monopolies Commission does not, however, have the right to question
the statutory monopolies granted to most, if not all,
the professions. Legal privileges are a professional
body's main source of power over its members, giving
weight to the threat of expulsion for failing to observe
its guidelines on 'professional practice'.

Recently an optician who advertised soft contact
lenses at the 'lowest price in England' and canvassed
for patients was struck off by the General Optical
Council, and the Privy Council dismissed his appeal.[2]
In any other branch of industry, this optician's actions
would be hailed as an example to all, and the General
Optical Council would be held to have acted against
the public interest. There is mounting evidence, both
here and in the USA, that such restrictions on advertising serve only to raise prices. The monopoly conferred
by the 1958 Opticians Act should therefore be repealed
forthwith, and the present restrictions on advertising
and publicity removed, as indeed was recommended in
the recent report by the Director General of Fair
Trading.

Critical attention ought also to be paid to the process
of creating new professions which invariably entails
restrictions of some kind. For example, the Insurance
Brokers Registration Act 1977 prevents anyone from
calling himself an insurance broker unless he belongs to
the relevant association (though as yet there is no re-
striction on the practice of insurance broking). The Life
Insurance Association is currently attempting to license
life-assurance salesmen. The creation of a professional
body is not objectionable *per se*, nor is the imposition of
professional standards for membership in that body, for

[2] *Birmingham Evening Mail*, 22 July 1982.

this may certainly be in the consumer's interest given his relative ignorance of technical matters. The danger arises when membership of a particular body becomes a legal requisite for providing a particular service, since this simultaneously deprives the consumer of an alternative source of supply and provides the conditions under which cartels are most apt to flourish.

Removing monopoly references on the professions from political decision

Another case in the news illustrates this danger. The Government has refused to recognise members of the Association of Authorised Accountants as qualified to audit company accounts. The Association's secretary is reported as commenting:

> 'It must now be alleged against the Government that they are fully determined to protect a closed shop on behalf of vested interests, in contradiction to the principles of the recent Bill in Parliament which stopped trades unions from perpetrating closed shops.'[3]

This view is entirely understandable. Bearing in mind the political pressures on the Secretary of State, it would seem desirable for the Director General himself to be given the power to refer to the Monopolies Commission any statutory monopoly pertaining to professional bodies, and also any proposal to modify these monopolies or create new ones.

[3] *The Times*, 20 August 1982.

3. TRADE UNIONS AND RESTRICTIVE LABOUR PRACTICES

In a recent review[4] of the present Government's performance to date, almost all the contributors, of varying political hues, identified trade unions as a major problem yet to be dealt with. Restrictive practices in the labour market were held to be one reason for Britain's poor economic performance and high rate of unemployment. Closed shops, secondary picketing, over-manning, demarcation agreements and so on were highlighted.

Ever since the 1973 Fair Trading Act, governments have had the power to refer to the Commission a specified 'restrictive labour practice', but no government has yet done so. This is an obvious direction for further investigation, but the political pressures are no doubt immense. Once again, it would seem sensible for the Director General himself to have the power to refer restrictive labour practices to the Commission for investigation.

It is by no means obvious that these restrictive practices are in the interests of trade union members. Consider, for instance, the agreements between unions not to 'poach' each other's members. If firms made such an agreement about their customers, it would generally (and rightly) be held to be against the interests of consumers, whom it would deprive of the protection of competition. Similarly, non-poaching agreements deprive workers of the protection of competition between unions. Unions can perform valuable functions in informing their members of levels of pay and working conditions in comparable jobs elsewhere, advising them

[4] *Could Do Better*, Occasional Paper 62, IEA, 1982.

on their terms of employment, representing them in wage bargaining, enforcing their legal rights, and so on. Is one to suppose that all unions are equally able in this respect, and that standards of performance would not improve if unions had actively to compete for members? At the very least, trade unions should have to set forth explicitly the case for their restrictive practices being *in* the public interest.

4. 'ANTI-COMPETITIVE' PRACTICES

The Competition Act 1980 empowers the Director-General to investigate whether a particular course of conduct amounts to an 'anti-competitive' practice, defined as 'restricting, distorting or preventing competition'. If he identifies an anti-competitive practice, he can refer it to the Commission to establish whether it is against the public interest.

The phrase 'anti-competitive' is somewhat misleading since it is entirely possible that a practice which restricts competition in *some* respects may stimulate competition in *others*. The problem is well illustrated by the first case investigated by the Commission, concerning TI Raleigh's refusal to supply bicycles to discount chains such as Argos.[5] Suppose a manufacturer refuses to supply a chain store on the grounds that desirable pre- or post-sales services will not be provided, or that the co-operation of his existing retail outlets will be reduced, or even that the brand image of his product will be jeopardised. There is no doubt that the manufacturer's conduct may limit the ability of the chain store to compete against other retailers who do receive supplies.

[5] Monopolies and Mergers Commission, *Bicycles*, H C Paper 67, Session 1981-2, HMSO, 1981.

Yet there is equally no doubt that the conduct in question may enhance the ability of the manufacturer to compete with the brands of other manufacturers. In other words, *refusal to supply may simultaneously be 'anti-competitive' in retailing but 'pro-competitive' in manufacturing*. It is therefore quite possible that, *on balance*, refusal to supply may actually *promote* competition in the aggregate supply of a particular product.

Similar remarks apply to other alleged anti-competitive practices such as tie-in sales, full-line forcing, retrospective discounts, exclusive dealing, and so on. The 1980 Act seems to reflect the once-prevalent view that these practices are predominantly devices for extending monopoly and restricting entry. Yet in the USA, this view is gradually giving way to a recognition that in many situations these practices are means of increasing efficiency or coping with uncertainty.[6]

Reducing scope and uncertainty

The flurry of anti-competitive investigations by the OFT highlights a potential problem. Since the 1980 Act requires the Director General merely to establish whether a course of conduct has *any* anti-competitive implications, *regardless* of its pro-competitive aspects, both the OFT and Commission will surely be inundated with much needless work. Thousands of firms will be uncertain whether their wide variety of actual or proposed practices will be investigated and found against the public interest. The Director General expects that a 'case law' will be established on anti-competitive practices (Annual Report 1980), but the Commission's

[6] Richard A. Posner, 'The Chicago School of Antitrust Analysis', *University of Pennsylvania Law Review*, Vol. 127, No. 4, April 1979, pp. 925-48.

previous record on monopoly and merger references suggests that this is unduly optimistic. Some means should therefore be sought for reducing the scope and uncertainty of the present approach.

One possibility would be for the OFT to ascertain whether a practice is anti-competitive *on balance* (i.e. after taking into account its pro-competitive aspects). Only in the event of such a finding could the Commission be required to consider whether the conduct was in the (wider) public interest. But this would mean the two investigations would duplicate each other even more than at present, there would be pressure for full hearings at both stages, and the time and cost of each case might be doubled.

A preferable alternative would be simply to prohibit the abuse of a dominant market position.[7] Admittedly it is not easy to define a dominant firm: the mere fact that a firm supplies 50 per cent of a particular market does not mean that it 'controls' that market, or even half of it. This approach would, however, have the advantage that the 'public interest' would not need to be addressed afresh in each investigation. A firm would be presumed to act against the public interest if, and only if, it engaged in a systematic pattern of conduct (not merely a single act) against a particular competitor, i.e. conduct designed to drive the competitor out of the market, or persuade it to 'fall into line', or dissuade a potential competitor from entering.

[7] M. E. Beesley, 'Mergers and Economic Welfare', in *Mergers, Takeovers and the Structure of Industry*, IEA Readings No. 10, 1977; J. F. Pickering, 'Notes on the Future of Competition Policy in the UK', Competition Policy Conference, Oxford Centre for Management Studies, 13-15 November 1981, at para. 32.

We may illustrate the concept of a systematic pattern of conduct from two recent OFT reports.[8] Scottish and Universal Newspapers were found to have put pressure on a printer not to publish a rival paper, launched their own free paper, given free advertising on condition that no space was taken in the rival paper, and sold their own advertising below cost. In contrast, British Rail's refusal to provide Motorail service to a parcel delivery company competing with its own Red Star service would not, as a single act, constitute a systematic pattern of anti-competitive conduct.

This approach would have the additional advantage that anti-competitive practices could be handled by the Courts (as in the USA and EEC) instead of by the Monopolies Commission. Aggrieved competitors as well as the Director General could bring cases to Court, thereby speeding up the procedure, providing more effective protection, and economising on the OFT's resources. This reform would also give stronger hopes for the establishment of reliable precedent.

5. DISSATISFACTION WITH MERGER POLICY

The major criticism of competition policy advanced by the SDP policy document concerns the appraisal of mergers. It observes that

> 'Under current legislation, the onus of proof is on the authorities to show that the takeover is bad. As a result, few takeovers get referred to the Monopolies Commission; even fewer are prevented.' (p. 18)

This is true. As Table I shows, over the four years

[8] Office of Fair Trading, *Scottish and Universal Newspapers Limited,* 11 January 1983, and *British Railways Board Allocation of Facilities on Motorail,* 9 February 1983.

TABLE I

MERGER CONTROL 1978-81

Size of Assets Acquired £ million	No. of Co.'s eligible for referral*	No. of Co.'s referred**	No. of mergers abandoned	No. of findings against public interest
0— 25	533 (339)	3	1	0
25— 50	116	3	0	1
50— 100	73	2	1	0
100— 250	54	2	1	2
250— 500	26	3	0	1
500—1,000	12	1	0	1
1,000 & over	18	0	0	0
	832 (638)	14	3	5

*Asset criterion increased from £5 million to £15 million in April 1980. Figures in parentheses show the number eligible if the £15 million criterion had applied throughout.

**Two separate bids for the same company are treated as one potential merger.

Source: Annual Reports of the Director General of Fair Trading, 1978-81, and relevant Monopolies and Mergers Commission reports.

1978-81, more than 832 potential mergers were eligible for referral to the Commission, but only 14 were actually referred, and only 5 of the referred mergers were subsequently found to be against the public interest. (The figures for 1982 are not yet available.)

The SDP policy document goes on to recommend that

'The onus of proof should be shifted. Takeovers over a certain size should be disallowed unless the companies can demonstrate that they will offer some net advantage to the public interest.'

The justification put forward for this change of approach is that

'Practical experience suggests that often takeovers produce disappointing results; they sometimes increase market power, and often dissipate management time and effort in organisational changes which have little or bad effect on efficiency.'

It is clear that the main justification put forward for stricter control of mergers is *not* that they will prejudice competition. Nor is any mention made of adverse consequences in other respects (e.g. for employment or exports). The justification is that mergers are a substitute for increased efficiency—a way of avoiding difficult problems—which often yield poor financial results. In short, it is proposed that the Commission's rules should be changed so that the Commission can protect the shareholder and the public against lazy and incompetent management.

The concept of an 'efficiency watchdog' is of course a familiar one. This kind of thinking lay behind the Prices and Incomes Board, the Prices Commission, the Industrial Reorganisation Corporation and the National

Enterprise Board, all of which have subsequently been abolished (or, in the case of the NEB, slowly castrated). However, if the logic of the 'proof of efficiency' argument is accepted for mergers, it is not clear where it should end. If appraisal of mergers is justified on the ground that it will protect the parties concerned from ill-conceived decisions, why not similarly insist on appraising all investment projects, bank loans and new capital flotations on the Stock Exchange? Should the companies involved in these activities be required to demonstrate some net advantage to the public interest before receiving permission to go ahead?

Arguments against the 'efficiency watchdog' approach
There are several reasons why this line of argument should not be accepted, nor the proposed change implemented.

First, the view that 'companies should grow by internal development, rather than merger and acquisition' is, quite simply, misconceived. If it is quicker and cheaper to buy an existing company's assets, this is the efficient way to grow. For example, Lloyds Bank would probably not have been able to compete in estate agency—and certainly not so soon—if it had been required to build up its own custom from scratch. Or again, if small companies are more effective at innovating and large companies more effective at exploiting innovations, it is more efficient for large companies to buy up small companies than to insist that they develop their own new products. What matters is whether the innovations are made and exploited, not whether companies are righteously self-sufficient.

Secondly, the statistical evidence on the unprofitability of mergers, although important and challenging, is by no means conclusive. The studies typically assume that profitability would otherwise have continued at the pre-merger level, but many mergers seem to take place precisely because the firms concerned do *not* expect this to be possible. Comparisons are also made with the trend of average profitability of others in the same industry, but insofar as mergers facilitate the elimination of excess capacity, or stimulate competitive responses, it is possible that they raise the profitability of the whole industry. The unprofitability of mergers may therefore have been over-estimated. It is also important to recognise that firms may merge in order to reduce the uncertainty of their environment, which may bring long-term benefits not reflected in short-term profits.

Thirdly, preventing mergers does nothing to increase management efficiency, and may indeed hinder the identification and elimination of inefficiencies. Thus, contrary to the Commission's intentions, the main beneficiaries of its negative verdicts are more likely to be the existing management and employees of those companies that would otherwise have been taken over, rather than the shareholders and customers of these companies, or the general public.

Finally, it is a delusion to believe that a Commission can effectively discriminate between those mergers which will be in the companies' own interests and those which will not. In an uncertain and ever-changing world, intuitive but undocumented hunches may be much more important than sophisticated probability analyses. No-one would claim that management is perfect, or that errors are not made. But it is scarcely plausible to believe that, on the basis of six months' part-time reading, an assortment of lawyers, businessmen, economists and trade unionists can make consistently better forecasts than those people presently or potentially engaged in running the businesses.

6. AN ALTERNATIVE CRITIQUE OF MERGER POLICY

The real problem of current UK merger policy is surely quite different. It is that the 'public interest' clause leads to arbitrary judgements which are often *at the expense of competition*. A secondary problem is that many firms suffer needlessly from the uncertainty and scope of the policy.

Requiring mergers to be appraised in terms of a vaguely-defined 'public interest' leads to unpredictable and inconsistent judgements, which often seem to depend upon the particular composition of the Commission panel. The split verdicts on the Royal Bank of Scotland and Chartered Consolidated cases exemplify this problem. There is no objective way of weighing the effects on future employment in Scotland (even supposing that these can be adequately predicted) against the effects on competition throughout Britain. In consequence, the public-interest clause gives full rein to political pressures and prejudices, not least from interested government departments at the referral stage and when consequential action is under consideration. All too often, the long-term interests of consumers take second place.

Reforming the Monopolies Commission's criteria

In order to focus the Commission's attention on issues of monopoly and competition, where its contribution is more useful, it seems necessary to modify the terms of reference. Suppose the Commission were required to determine

(a) whether competition is affected by a proposed merger, and

(b) if it is *adversely* affected (e.g. restricted or distorted in some way), whether this is on balance against the interests of consumers.

The onus would then be on the Minister to overturn this judgement (on 'political' grounds). Before doing so, he might wish to refer a particular matter back to the Commission (e.g. to assess whether regional employment would be significantly affected).

It would be desirable explicitly to eliminate from consideration those mergers unlikely to be found against the public interest. Approximately 150 mergers per year are eligible for referral but are not in practice referred. Some, of course, are never likely to be referred, but for many firms there must be a period of considerable uncertainty. Furthermore, investigation itself may impose a substantial burden—not merely the time and expense of being investigated but also the potentially damaging consequences of having to reveal confidential information about assets and plans, and the fact that opportunities dependent upon current relative stock market prices may disappear during (or as a result of) the six-months investigation.

To minimise such problems, the assets referral criterion should be substantially increased. The Table suggests that, if the criterion were raised, over 500 mergers eligible for referral over the four years 1978-81 would have been exempt, but only one merger subsequently found against the public interest would have escaped investigation. Some 30 mergers per year would still require OFT appraisal.

These figures are necessarily conjectural since the effect of the market share criterion cannot be deduced from the Table. For simplicity, this criterion has not been used in recent years. Previous definitions of the relevant market have also (and rightly) been criticised for their narrowness (e.g. white fish in the Humber ports, or men's suits under £20). There are no 'correct' figures or definitions, but an increase in the market share referral criterion, from 25 to 33 per cent or even 50 per cent, would help to ensure that this criterion is only called upon where significant monopoly power is likely to be entailed.

Abandon ex ante *merger control?*

Whether these modifications in merger policy would suffice is admittedly debateable. It is hard enough for the Commission to identify and evaluate the 'things done' in a monopoly or anti-competitive practices reference. To predict what *might* be done as a result of a merger makes *ex ante* cost-benefit analysis almost impossibly difficult. Changing the Commission's terms of reference will facilitate the analysis of the effects on competition, and raising the referral criteria will focus attention on the most important cases. Nevertheless, the system is still vulnerable to error and political pressures.

Several commentators are beginning to question the whole idea of *ex ante* appraisal of potential mergers.[9] Instead, emphasis might be placed on the prevention or elimination of any subsequent anti-competitive conduct through the abuse of a dominant position. This further

[9] *Cf.* Beesley and Pickering, *op. cit.* (above, note 7).

move to an 'effects-based' policy is consistent with the earlier suggestions on anti-competitive practices (p. 97), and deserves further investigation, but there is not space to do this here.

7. NATIONALISED INDUSTRIES

The SDP policy towards nationalised industries is set out at some length in the *Industrial Strategy* document (pp. 29-34). It may be summarised as follows:

(1) What matters is the extent to which the nationalised industries are operated efficiently, are sufficiently responsive to the needs of consumers, and meet their social obligations.

(2) All the nationalised industries should be exposed to stronger competitive forces wherever possible.

(3) There is no objection to private shareholdings in competitive nationalised industries, but the question of ownership is of little interest in its own right, and switching ownership backwards and forwards could ruin the industries.

(4) In the absence of competitive forces, an Efficiency Audit Commission (EAC) should be established for the nationalised industries; a system of Supervisory Boards should provide more independence and ensure implementation of the EAC's recommendations; and 'External Finance Limits' should ensure that adequate finance is available.

The objectives in (1) are entirely reasonable—but how far will the measures in (2) to (4) achieve them? The endorsement of competition in (2) should be warmly commended. The other recommendations (3) and (4) are more problematical.

Neither the economic theory of public choice, nor UK experience to date, suggests that governments are willing or able to allocate investment funds on efficiency grounds; or to refrain from intervening in the running of the nationalised industries when it is politically expedient to do so. A number of efficiency audits have already been carried out by the MMC, mainly under the 1980 Competition Act. They appear to be thorough and fair, and to contain useful information and suggestions.[10] But are such audits likely to be effective in actually increasing efficiency? Suppose, as envisaged by the Act, that the Secretary of State 'orders the preparation of a plan to remedy the situation'. Is there any guarantee that this plan will be implemented? What is the sanction for non-compliance?

Consumers can be effectively protected against inefficiency only by the force of competition. The SDP recognises this truth, but thinks that 'the opportunities for introducing competition into nationalised industries are much less than many people think'. This is too pessimistic; my hunch is that precisely the opposite is the case. Take the SDP's own example: it argues that splitting British Telecom's international services from its domestic services would not expose them to more intensive market pressures. But it *would*—because each of the two independent companies so formed would seek protection from the other by encouraging new entry to compete with its sole supplier or customer. There is no doubt that competition can be significantly increased in *all* the nationalised industries, especially with the rapid development of new technology. We should therefore attempt to remove the present artificial

[10] B. Chiplin and M. Wright, 'Competition Policy and State Enterprises in the UK', *Antitrust Bulletin*, Winter 1982.

barriers to new entry and to re-structure the industries with the aim of promoting competition, before worrying overmuch about the lack of scope for doing so.

A stronger competition policy, such as outlined earlier, will have an important rôle to play. Vigilance against anti-competitive practices, so as to protect new or small competitors against possible abuse of the dominant positions currently held by the nationalised industries, will *ipso facto* protect consumers.

Tariff restrictions—such as the RPI-X formula recently adopted for British Telecom's local services—may also be useful. But, as I have argued elsewhere,[11] this restraint is essentially a short-term safeguard to 'hold the fort' until competition arrives, rather than a permanent method of control.

The importance of private ownership

The SDP's lack of enthusiasm for a transfer to private ownership is understandable, since most members have come from the Labour Party. But is it sensible? Consider the following four points:

(i) There is extensive and growing empirical evidence, mainly from the USA, that private ownership increases efficiency, output and innovation.

(ii) Competition alone has not been sufficient to ensure that nationalised industries such as British Airways, BL and British Steel have been run profitably or efficiently.

(iii) It is questionable whether the recent increased competition in telecommunications would have

[11] *Regulation of British Telecommunications' Profitability*, Department of Industry, HMSO, February 1983.

been *politically* feasible had not the transfer of BT to private ownership already been proposed.

(iv) It is arguable that competition policy is (and certainly could be) more effective against a private company than against a nationalised industry.

This is not to suggest that privatisation is free of difficulties, and in certain industries (such as electricity distribution) it would not be the first priority. Nonetheless, the transfer from public to private ownership should not be lightly dismissed; rather, it should be regarded as an integral part of a policy to ensure efficiency by increasing competition.[12]

8. CONCLUSIONS

SDP policy is to develop a vigorous private business sector and to promote competition, as means to increase efficiency and growth, which in turn are necessary to create jobs and a fair society. In this paper I have supported the call for more competition, but argued that certain suggestions are misconceived—specifically, the proposal to place the onus of proof of social benefit on merging companies, and the proposed Efficiency Audit Commission for nationalised industries. SDP policy would place a heavier burden on governments and commissions than they can realistically sustain, and inadequate account is taken of the

---

[12] For further discussion of privatisation, S. C. Littlechild, 'Ten Steps to Denationalisation', *Journal of Economic Affairs*, Vol. 2, No.1, October 1981; M. E. Beesley and S. C. Littlechild, 'Privatisation: Principles, Problems and Priorities', *Lloyds Bank Review*, July 1983.

political pressures which will inevitably be brought to bear.

My own suggestions are for a different change in emphasis in competition policy. Legislation on restrictive practices has proved relatively successful, and should be extended to services and labour markets, with the Director General given power to initiate references. Anti-competitive practices legislation should be focused on abuse of a dominant position by systematic conduct aimed at a particular rival; this function could be transferred from the Monopolies Commission to the Courts. The terms of reference on mergers should be modified so that the Commission would assess whether competition is adversely affected, with the onus placed on the Minister to overturn this judgement if public interest/political considerations so dictate. The reference criteria should also be raised to eliminate the smaller firms from the net. In the longer term, consideration should be given to abandoning *ex ante* merger control altogether. Finally, competition can and should be increased throughout the nationalised industries, by removing barriers to entry and re-structuring existing organisations. Privatisation would be an integral part of this competitive programme.

In sum, the SDP is right to exphasise the importance of competition, but the attempt to design commissions to act as *substitutes* for competition is counter-productive. The greatest benefits are to be secured by allowing competition into those markets which have hitherto been protected from it, and by reducing the scope for political pressures to jeopardise the actual conduct of competition policy.

SEVEN

EMPLOYEE PARTICIPATION AND THE PROMOTION OF EMPLOYEE OWNERSHIP

Ljubo Sirc

University of Glasgow

The Author

LJUBO SIRC: born in Yugoslavia in 1920. During the Second World War he took part in the resistance and also graduated in economics and law from the University of Ljubljana in 1943. He escaped to Switzerland to report on occupied Yugoslavia and joined Tito's army of liberation by a roundabout journey through France. He was arrested in 1947 by the Yugoslav government for conspiracy against the State, and imprisoned.

He escaped to Italy in 1955 and made his way to Britain, where he worked as a BBC monitor. In 1960 he took a doctorate in economics at Fribourg University in Switzerland and thereafter spent a year lecturing at the University of Dacca, East Bengal. Since 1962 he has been a lecturer in international economics, first at the University of St Andrews, and, since 1965, at the University of Glasgow. His publications include: *The Yugoslav Economy under Self-management* (Macmillan, London, and St. Martin's Press, New York, 1979); 'The Position of the Industrial Enterprise in Yugoslavia' in I. Jeffries (ed.), *The Industrial Enterprise in Eastern Europe* (Holt-Saunders/Praeger Special, 1981); and numerous articles on Eastern Europe and international economics in specialist journals. The IEA published his 'State Control and Competition in Yugoslavia', in *Communist Economy under Change* (1963), *Economic Devolution in Eastern Europe* (1969), and 'Workers' Management under Public and Private Ownership' in *Can Workers Manage?* (Hobart Paper 77, 1977).

Employee Participation and the Promotion of Employee Ownership

1. THE END OF ENTREPRENEURSHIP?

Forty years ago, Joseph Schumpeter thought that he was witnessing the demise of entrepreneurship. In his *Capitalism, Socialism and Democracy*, he wrote that

> 'the function of entrepreneurs is to reform or revolutionise the pattern of production by exploiting an invention or, more generally, an untried technical possibility for producing a new commodity or producing an old one in a new way, by opening a new source of supply of materials or a new outlet for products, by reorganising an industry and so on.'

But then he thought he saw

> 'innovation itself being reduced to routine. Technological progress is increasingly becoming the business of teams of trained specialists who turn out what is required and make it work in predictable ways. The romance of earlier commercial adventure is rapidly wearing away, because so many more things can be strictly calculated that had of old to be visualised in a flash of genius.'[1]

Thus there was no need any more for people who combined innate gifts with considerable technical (though not academic) knowledge, not to say feeling,

---

[1] Joseph Schumpeter, *Capitalism, Socialism and Democracy*, Unwin University Books, 1954; 5th Edn., Allen & Unwin, 1976, p. 132.

113

and commercial daring. All their functions would be taken over by bureaucrats and technocrats. These passages were written in 1942, when the admiration for the Russian resistance to the Nazi invasion became reflected in a high opinion of the Soviet system of economic planning, about the actual results of which very little was known. In this atmosphere, even an economist of Schumpeter's standing could be misled into believing that the deeds of the entrepreneur had been done.

When the war was over, an era of unprecedented and unexpected economic growth followed, interspersed with attempts at economic planning even in market economies. By the mid-1960s, however, the strictly planned economies in Eastern Europe were overwhelmed by a sense of futility—all their wheels were turning furiously allegedly generating high growth rates but adding disproportionately little to the well-being of their populations. Reforms, actually introducing market elements in some countries, were on the agenda although regarded with suspicion by Communist authorities and finally suppressed. Most countries returned to the greyness of 'socialist' life which was interrupted by the open revolt in Poland in 1980.

The only country in the Soviet sphere enjoying some kind of fool's freedom in the way of running the economy was—and remains—Hungary, which did introduce useful reforms, but of late came to the conclusion that the reform that would really matter would be to find some way of introducing 'socialist entrepreneurship'. Is it perhaps not true that enough things can now be strictly calculated to dispense with talented men with special insights? More than that: Is it perhaps necessary to have clearly defined responsibilities for managing an enterprise even when no spectacular innovation is involved?

Yugoslavia's experiment with 'self-managed enterprises'

Yugoslavia went a somewhat different way after having initially introduced a Soviet-type system. When Stalin expelled Tito from the socialist camp, the Yugoslav Communist party hit on the idea of self-management to counter the Soviet ideological onslaught. While it was originally combined with centrally-planned investment, it became obvious that investment planning by political bodies produced 'political factories'. It was therefore decided to entrust this so called 'expanded reproduction' to self-managed enterprises, expecting that their 'self-managers' would collectively behave as entrepreneurs.

Yugoslavia's new arrangements misfired so badly that her economic chaos in 1983 is no better than and no different from that in the rest of Eastern Europe. Some Yugoslav economists now see clearly that the bad final result could have been foreseen on the basis of simple economic tenets. Whilst more will be said later about these foreseeable shortcomings, the gist of the argument is that workers in factories cannot be made interested in placing capital where it is most productive.

Two solutions are suggested: first, that Yugoslavia should return to 'programmed' investment which has failed before. Secondly, that the motivation of workers should be improved (but nobody knows how) so that they would perform the entrepreneurial function which is currently not undertaken by anyone, and the absence of which—*pace* Schumpeter—has led to economic chaos.

2. WESTERN DESIRE FOR DEMOCRACY AT WORK

In Western Europe the post-war era was marked by half-hearted moves in almost the same direction as in Stalin's Soviet Union, e.g. by nationalisations in Britain and planning in France. Both the Western experience with these policies and the spreading inefficiency in Eastern Europe have, however, reduced the attraction of such measures. Nonetheless, they have not yet disappeared from the programmes of some parties, though nobody can by now seriously expect the application of such policies to solve any human or economic problems.

As a consequence, the ground has shifted. The road to Utopia envisaged by intellectual ideologists now winds up another hill. Many enthuse about the 30 years of Yugoslav self-management, though with much more admiration than knowledge. Some people clearly think that entrepreneurs can simply be replaced by voting collectives; few realise that it is precisely the impossibility of such substitution that makes the Yugoslav system shake in its foundations.

Success of German works' councils—'co-determination'

On the other hand, there is the Central European tradition of works' councils which stood godmother to the Federal German works' councils instituted soon after the war. The success of the West Germany economy, which may have had something to do with these councils but which was also encouraged by other favourable circumstances, made the idea of workers' 'parliaments' in enterprises popular—in the event so popular that their proposed jurisdiction was pushed well beyond its original limits. In Germany itself, the 1976 Act on 'Co-determination' widened the powers of workers' representatives into new areas, but is still considered by many as simply a stepping-stone towards what Proudhon called 'workshops without masters'.[2] From a down-to-earth working arrangement, the election of workers' representatives has been elevated to a question of democracy at work.

This direction of ideological requests is a new turn in the thinking of intellectuals. So far social criticism has been directed mainly at the distribution of income. Critics objected to the market economy because it produced a pattern of personal incomes of which they did not approve, especially since they were not commensurate with the apparent work-effort. It was also claimed that spontaneous markets were chaotic and should be replaced by conscious planning, the rather sad results of which have already been mentioned. Under this first socialist solution, it could hardly be said that working individuals were less subject to orders from above than under capitalism, except that the ordering was done by other people.

The failure of planning and nationalisations did not so much put us on a different tack as to multiply the tacks. Now the critics want a different distribution of income, but they also want the cutting of bosses down to size. It is said that there is no reason why people who are free citizens and electors in political life should not enjoy democratic rights at their place of work. More than that: work should be self-fulfilment for workers.

[2] Pierre Proudhon (1809-65), *Systèmes des contradictions économique ou philosophie de la misère*, 1848.

Self-sustaining enthusiasm for 'democracy'
and 'self-fulfilment'

The slogans of 'democracy' and 'self-fulfilment' are, not surprisingly, very catching, and have attracted followers from much further afield than the usual circle of Utopian schemers. What is more, industrial democracy does not seem to disturb market relationships, and this appeals to moderates who want change but distrust planning since the resulting chaos is all too noticeable. For the more 'advanced' social thinkers, however, even the market is a restraint of self-fulfilment and should be done away with, so that the workers can produce 'freely'. At this stage, the present author completely loses the hang of the argument.

At any rate, by now the economics of the matter—the question of efficiency—has been pushed to one side and enthusiasm has taken over about what wonderful things are going to happen when everybody decides about everything himself in conjunction with everybody else. Lots of heat is generated and an atmosphere has been created in which it is not advisable to talk about the difficulties. The present author knows of at least one German University which was not prepared to publish a critical lecture and of at least one occasion when a discussion of co-determination had to be called off because neither the trade unions nor the employees were ready to discuss practical issues.

That is why this question has to be put on the Social Democratic agenda. Social democrats as persons who care about people will want to do what they can to promote people's well-being. But they then have to read carefully what has been discovered about industrial democracy so far and answer the awkward questions rather than sweep them under the carpet.

3. INDUSTRIAL DEMOCRACY

The Oxford Dictionary defines democracy as 'that form of government in which the sovereign power resides in the people'. The most adequate translation of 'sovereign' in less technical terms is 'supreme' and it seems obvious that there can be only one supreme power or body in the same territory. There were long discussions about whether in federal states there could be divided sovereignty and the general conclusion was that this division was possible provided the two jurisdictions were neatly separated and there was a court to pronounce on disputes. Units at even lower levels than constituent parts of a federation are not sovereign but autonomous, which means that the sovereign body determines the aims they should pursue and the limits within which they can do so.

There cannot be much doubt that the sovereign body, if asked what the goal of a commercial enterprise should be, would answer in line with economic tenets that it is to produce goods people want at the cheapest possible price, i.e. with the least use of resources. Once this is decided, the managing of an enterprise becomes mainly technical, i.e. concerned with the question of what means to use to achieve the goal. The solution of this task depends on knowledge, information, experience, innate talent, and so on, rather than on whether the majority votes for it or not. In this respect, decision-making in an enterprise resembles more the work of an engineer or medical doctor than that of a politician who is essentially concerned with value-judgements, i.e., pronouncements on what people want to achieve. There does not seem, therefore, to be much scope for democracy in industry.

The primacy of workers as consumers

The difference from purely technical work is, of course, that industrial decision-makers are involved with large numbers of people and must obtain their co-operation. But this cannot possibly mean that the enterprises should be run exclusively in the interest of their workers as producers, or that everything should be done to meet their wishes. Enterprises must also and primarily be run in the interest of workers as consumers, otherwise the wages of workers as producers would become use-less and the whole system would break down. If the workers as producers work less or in ways which reduce efficiency by more than they are prepared to lose as consumers, they must in the final analysis come into conflict with themselves. It is true that this relationship is masked by the intermediary rôle of entrepreneurs-industrial organisers, but this intermediate step does not render it unimportant. Marxism has done considerable harm by making light of this basic connection and by pretending that it is, so to speak, fully severed by entrepreneurs whom it decries as exploiters even though they have contributed most to the present material prosperity.

Yet another difference between technical work and economic organisation is of crucial importance. Enterprise decisions, particularly those on investment, are taken under conditions of uncertainty, which means that they entail subjective assessments of future develop-ments in demand, technology and factor supply. Thus they can be no more than informed guesses, highly skilled hunches the only check on which is the end-result. Hence they imply risk-taking. This special quality of enterprise decisions does not make it easy to convert them into collective decision-making by voting.

The conclusion must be that it is in all probability a misunderstanding of democracy to want to introduce it in enterprises as a reflection of democracy at the national level; and it is a misunderstanding of entrepreneurial decisions to want them to be taken by democratic procedures.

Democratic rights and duties

Democracy can, of course, be understood in a different way, in the sense of respect for human individuals as enshrined in the democratic protection of human rights. Certainly this respect for people should not be practised exclusively by legislatures, but by people themselves in their relationships with each other. However, it then requires that rights and respect should be mutual, which seems also to imply that rights should be matched by duties. 'Duties' primarily means duties towards the community; in fact, translated into the terminology of this article, it could be said that workers as producers should not be a law unto themselves but should bear in mind that they also have interests as consumers, and this interest requires efficient production. Some democratic civility should, moreover, be spared also for entrepreneurs who are now all too often treated as 'class enemies' while in fact they are the decisive link in material progress.

Finally, it is not by chance that, at the political level, the collective democratic might is required to be tempered by the rights of individuals. Similarly, if some room is not reserved for the creative power of individuals in the economy, the pace of economic progress will be slowed down to the speed, or lack of speed, of the slowest.

4. DECISIONS ON CAPITAL

While the appropriateness of democratic decisions in enterprises is questionable in general, it can be demonstrated that such decisions are harmful when applied to capital which is not owned by the decision-makers; they are harmful for the workers themselves as consumers and they are harmful for workers as producers. Doubts are justified about whether full-time workers have either the time or the inclination to take decisions on capital in their spare time because economic decision-making requires not simply voting but also, and more importantly, the time-consuming business of absorbing the information required to reach those decisions. Even if decision-making is entrusted to workers' representatives who are instructed to act in the interests of the workers in an enterprise, the results will still be harmful.

The reason is very simple: it is in the interests of workers to raise their own productivity by combining as much capital with their own labour as will still add something to their output, because this addition raises their wages. This wish does not take into account the need to invest capital where it yields most and thus spread it all over the economy so that the wages of workers as a whole will be maximised. What is more, concentration of capital in some enterprises and with some workers must cause unemployment or at least lack of capital elsewhere. The result is exactly the same as when workers simply demand excessively high wages. Entrepreneurs must then substitute capital for labour in order to pay such wages and, as a consequence, there is not enough capital to create jobs for everybody.

Further, there is no possibility of making workers

responsible for decisions on capital which they do not own since they cannot take the original decision of investing capital to start new jobs, since they are new jobs, and since the composition of workers in an enterprise changes all the time, so that some decision-making workers will no longer be there when the consequences of a decision show up.

Any 'participation' which gives non-owners of capital jurisdiction over its deployment must in the end be harmful to the workers themselves because it is bound to lead to irrational decisions. The Yugoslav system of self-management has shown this clearly after 30 years' experience. Some observers of the German scene predict that the German parity co-determination will yield similar results,[3] but it seems that it takes a long time before the bad results hit the economy with their full force; in addition, parity co-determination is only a partial influence on investment, of course, but insofar as it is an influence it makes no economic sense.

Can workers be turned into owners successfully?

The solution to these criticisms—that decision-making by non-owners of capital must have bad consequences —may be to turn the workers into owners. How might this change of ownership be brought about? There already exist all kinds of plans for fostering ownership by employees which seem rather artificial. If a person obtains capital ownership as manna from heaven, it seems unlikely that the simple transfer of ownership

[3] Gerhard Prosi, *Volkswirtschaftliche Auswirkungen des Mitbestimmungsgesetzes 1976 (Effects of the 1976 Act on Co-determination on the National Economy)*, Otto A. Friedrich-Kuratorium, Cologne, 1978.

will elicit entrepreneurial effort, let alone entrepreneurial talent, from him.

Besides, spreading ownership so thinly gives income from capital little weight as compared with income from work, so that presumably almost the same attitudes will prevail as with non-owners. People owning little capital will, moreover, not lose much sleep over how to invest it.

In all probability, a large part of such capital will end up in the hands of institutional investors who will distort capital markets when dominant and spread the investment risk so thinly that it no longer matters for individuals; mistakes will simply make the economy as a whole more inefficient. If the trade unions begin to administer capital, as is suggested in some countries, the right to dispose of it will become so concentrated and the capital markets so distorted that they will have to draw up investment plans. Even if they do this with the optimum solution in mind, they may not succeed in achieving this result any better than the East European governments. Things might get even worse if the purpose is to serve the interests of employees in the narrow sense, i.e. to prevent closures and reduce unemployment without paying attention to capital yields, because capital will then of necessity be deployed irrationally.

Can limited liability companies be reformed?

Instead of planning this kind of re-distribution of capital, we would be more usefully employed if we re-examined the rôle of limited companies.[4] While they

[4] Jo Grimond, 'Pity the poor shareholders', *Daily Telegraph*, 5 October 1981, p. 14.

have certainly played a useful part in the past, they now spread risk so much that it no longer matters, they transfer management into the hands of people who are largely independent of shareholders, and they allow companies to grow to a size which can no longer be defended on economic grounds. This ultimate distortion makes the failure of some companies so socially disruptive that governments are prepared to spend large sums to prevent it, and thus interfere with the normal course of economic progress.

On the whole, plans for participation in profits and re-distribution of wealth disregard the fact that both ownership and profits have an economic function which cannot be performed if they are artificially altered. In these circumstances they might just as well be abolished altogether. In addition, such changes raise the question of equity as between groups of workers, because employees in enterprises with larger profits will have higher incomes for no other reason than that in these enterprises there is more capital per worker.

5. CO-OPERATION BY CONTRACT AND ACCESS TO INFORMATION

The experience of the last 40 years suggests that the most successful form of participation has been the original German (and Central European) works' councils. In practice, they were not 'participation' in the full sense of the word but representation of workers so that capital-managers and workers' representatives could exchange views and information. This relationship should perhaps be developed further so that workers (possibly divided into smaller groups than the entire workforce in an enterprise) might conclude contracts with capital-managers to provide specific services and organise the work themselves. In this way there could be market relationships within the enterprise itself instead of set work according to instructions by managers. This would bring us nearer to what Proudhon seems to have envisaged when he suggested that economic activity should be based on contracts instead of subordination.

This arrangement may possibly have more scope than co-operatives which have always been legally possible but have never spread or prospered. Workers would have to organise themselves into teams which would perform certain work 'packages' without interference except for the initial specification of what was to be done and for what price. The risk which the workers have never been keen to take upon themselves would continue to fall on capital and its owners, who would have to invest, buy the inputs and sell the output.

Finally, when it comes to the desire for more information, it is important that the information imparted to workers should not be merely the data on the working of individual enterprises and on their profits and losses but information on how the whole economy works. Only when the workers are disabused of the notion that entrepreneurs are out to cheat and exploit them and are made to understand that entrepreneurs' main function is to organise efficient production, in which they have been singularly successful, will economic co-operation get underway again with most desirable results for the workers themselves. Even if some entrepreneurs only seek quick profits, the market economy on the whole forces them to pay the best possible wages.

One thing is certain: the capitalist enterprise does

produce the goods people want, which does not seem to be true of 'enterprises' either in planned economies or under self-management. The market economy may currently be beset by unemployment, but in the post-war world unemployment has become acute only since the 1970s, while earlier there was little to speak of and the Western economies grew at unprecedented rates. What if unemployment has something to do with the fact that in recent times entrepreneurs have no longer been allowed to get on with their jobs and enterprises have been faced with demands for wages which may be possible tomorrow, but if demanded today prevent tomorrow from arriving at all?

EIGHT

THE POST-WAR ECONOMIC FAILURE
OF BRITISH GOVERNMENT:
A PUBLIC CHOICE PERSPECTIVE

Charles K. Rowley

University of Newcastle upon Tyne

The Author

CHARLES K. ROWLEY was born in 1939 and educated at King Edward VI School, Southampton, and University of Nottingham (1st Class Honours 1960; PhD 1964). Since 1972 he has been the David Dale Professor of Economics, and since 1974 Director of the Centre for Research in Public and Industrial Economics at the University of Newcastle upon Tyne. Formerly taught at the Universities of Nottingham (1962-65), Kent (1965-70), and York (1970-72). He has been Visiting Professor at the Virginia Polytechnic Institute and State University, Blacksburg (1974 and 1979), and Emory University, Atlanta (1982).

He is the author of *The British Monopolies Commission* (1966); *Steel & Public Policy* (1971); *Antitrust and Economic Efficiency* (1972); (with A. T. Peacock) *Welfare Economics: A Liberal Restatement* (1975); *A Study of Effluent Discharges to the River Tees* (1978); 'The Political Economy of the Public Sector', in B. Jones (ed.), *Perspectives on Political Economy* (1982); 'Industrial Policy in the Mixed Economy', in Lord Roll of Ipesden (ed.), *The Mixed Economy* (1982). Editor of *International Review of Law and Economics*. For the IEA he contributed essays in *Catch '76 . . .?* (Occasional Paper 'Special', No. 47, 1976), *The Economics of Politics* (Readings 18, 1978), *The Myth of Social Cost* (Hobart Paper 82, 1978), and others.

The Post-War Economic Failure of British Government: A Public Choice Perspective

1. INTRODUCTION

The rate of economic growth of the United Kingdom over the 37 years since the end of the Second World War—measured in Gross National Product (GNP) per head of population—has been below that of any advanced economy within the Western world and spectacularly below that of Japan and West Germany. Against this national backcloth is the growth of state intervention in the UK economy, epitomised by the relentless growth of the public sector. As Table 1 indicates, the process continues quite independently of the political party in office.

Government expenditure, as defined in Table 1, includes local as well as central government outlays and reflects social security transfers within the UK. It excludes transfers by British governments to the rest of the world. Thus, although the measure over-states public sector output (narrowly defined), and although it is sensitive to recession, it remains the best single measure of the extent of government control over resources. It is perhaps especially worthy of note that government expenditure as a ratio of Gross Domestic Product (GDP) in 1981-82 exceeded that imposed by the Labour Government in 1976. Reductions in the ratio outlined from 1982 onwards are merely government forecasts.

TABLE I

THE GROWTH OF PUBLIC EXPENDITURE IN
BRITAIN: 1950 TO 1984-85

	Government Expenditure as a Ratio of Gross Domestic Product
	%
1950	30·2
1960	30·8
1970	35·5
1976	52·0
1977	43·6
1980-81	47·0
1981-82*	53·0
1982-83*	47·0
1983-84*	43·6
1984-85*	47·0

*Government forecasts.

Source: *Economic Progress Report 143*, HM Treasury, March
1982, and *National Income and Expenditure Accounts*
(Blue Books).

Such a pattern has not been evident at all times in
the economic history of this country. Indeed, a marked
stability is evident in the ratio between government
expenditure and GDP over the larger part of its recorded
history. In 1790, for example, the total expenditure of
the public authorities in Britain accounted for approximately 12 per cent of GNP. Some 120 years later, in
1913—despite substantial increases in government expenditures—the ratio of total government expenditure
to GNP was exactly the same, at 12 per cent.

2. THE ECONOMIC CASE FOR THE PROVISION OF COMMODITIES BY GOVERNMENT

For economists who work with Paretian welfare economics, the case for some form of government intervention, whether in legislation, tax/subsidy policies or direct regulation, appears manifold. Market failure may well arise as a consequence of externalities, monopolies, uncertainty, etc., even where the 'willingness-to-pay principle', based on the existing distribution of income and wealth, is endorsed. In addition, government intervention may be justified to correct perceived 'injustices' in the existing distribution of rights. The Paretian case for *public provision* of goods and services is altogether more restricted, resting upon the presence of pronounced 'publicness' characteristics in the commodities concerned.

Public goods—those that are characterised by both non-exclusivity and non-excludability in consumption—are comparatively rare in all societies. The property of non-exclusivity implies that the opportunity cost of individual consumption, once the commodity is available, is zero, with the efficiency implication that no individual should be excluded from its use, i.e., that the price should be zero. But private markets cannot exist with positive costs and zero revenues. Non-excludability implies that there is no economically viable technique whereby those who do not pay can be denied access to benefits, in which case, predictably, 'free-riders' will dominate and the facility will either not be provided at all or on an inefficiently small scale. In combination, these characteristics require public provision, if any such provision is justified.

How much of the public sector is public goods?

It is instructive to analyse the UK public sector, excluding all social security-type transfer payments, to determine the proportion of expenditure which takes the form of public good provision. Following a categorisation developed by Arthur Seldon,[1] only 21 per cent of government expenditures in 1974, *excluding* transfers, satisfied fully the public-good criteria (essentially military defence, civil defence, external relations, Parliament, the law courts, the prisons, public health, land drainage, coast protection, finance, tax collection, and a range of central government services). At the other extreme, the government spent in that year some 59 per cent of its total expenditure, excluding transfers, on commodities with entirely separable benefits, where full privatisation would satisfy Paretian efficiency requirements (essentially education, health, personal social services, school milk, meals and welfare foods, employment services, libraries, museums and art galleries, housing, water, sewage and refuse disposal, and transport and communications). These statistics ignore the nationalised industries, all of which are privatisable, albeit with safeguards where monopoly power exists (rare once commodity substitutes are correctly defined). Nor have these statistics been changed significantly by the trivial privatisation measures introduced since 1979.

Clearly, a considerable divergence exists in the UK between the relatively small percentage of GDP that welfare economics suggests can be provided by government and the much larger percentage which government does provide. It is the central message of this

[1] *Charge*, Maurice Temple Smith, London, 1977.

paper that much of the divergence is to be explained by public choice analysis.

3. THE PUBLIC CHOICE PERSPECTIVE

For the most part, even now, economists of neo-classical, utilitarian persuasion present policy recommendations on the basis of apparent market failure as if these would be implemented efficiently by an impartial, far-sighted government motivated by Paretian ideals. Such an approach is naïve.

Once it is recognised that the political process is a market place, in which policies and votes are traded by agents motivated by self-interest, a more satisfactory understanding of the growth and composition of the public sector emerges. Vote-seeking coalitions of politicians, pressed by organised interest groups of producers and consumers, and advised by bureaux dedicated to the pursuit of their own objectives, are unlikely systematically to implement policies that satisfy the conditions of Pareto-efficiency, even when such policies are clearly identifiable. Divergences from efficiency are further to be expected, once uncertainty is acknowledged in both the preferences of individual citizens on public provision and the appropriate mechanisms for translating divergent individual preferences into collective outcomes.

Two approaches

In essence, there are two approaches to the analysis of public choice, which rely not upon the altruistic, efficiency assumption of government but upon the self-seeking nature of agents engaged in the political process.

The first, *spatial analysis*, is relatively abstract in nature and arguably of limited value in understanding the political process. The second, *the institutional approach*, is more powerful and is revolutionising analysis of the political process.

(i) *Spatial analysis*

The spatial approach, first introduced by Downs[2] in 1957, centres attention upon political parties and their response to vote pressures and vote pressures alone. In principle, this approach is promising, at least when certain important assumptions hold. Specifically, if the policy-issue dimension can be defined clearly, if voter preferences are 'unimodal' (i.e. cluster round one 'peak'), if all voters vote, and if two parties compete for votes at all times, a unique equilibrium exists at the median (half way along) of the voter preference distribution. This result holds even when the voter preference distribution is highly skewed (i.e. where substantial differences exist between the mode (the most common preference), the median and the mean (the arithmetic average). The literature on spatial political analysis heralds this result as a breakthrough. Once these stringent assumptions are relaxed, however, the spatial model is less decisive and less useful in explaining government behaviour.

(ii) *The institutional approach*

The institutional approach attempts to analyse the behaviour of incumbent governments and oppositions, not merely at the point of the election process, but

[2] Anthony Downs, *An Economic Theory of Democracy*, Harper and Row, New York, 1957.

throughout the expected life in and out of office, within the constraints of the constitution they inherit, and subject to all the self-seeking pressures to which they are exposed. To the extent that institutions differ from economy to economy, the predictions of the institutional approach will tend to be restricted to the systems from which they have been generated. To the extent that institutional models offer superior predictions, however, the price of lost generality may be considered well worthwhile.

4. PUBLIC CHOICE AND THE MACRO-ECONOMIC FAILURE OF POST-WAR BRITISH GOVERNMENTS

Post-war British governments have exercised macro-economic policy in the absence of a written Constitution, essentially as a unicameral legislature, with internal disciplinary procedures designed to maximise party solidarity in the voting lobbies. The method of voting itself—first-past-the-post—is designed to preserve a two-party system. In such circumstances, the monopoly theory of government is relevant for much of post-war British politics, with opposition parties playing a trivial rôle except as election dates approach.

In macro-economic policy, post-war British governments have found themselves unfettered by two previously unwritten rules, both of which had constrained the behaviour of their predecessors for over 100 years. The first such rule, the gold standard, limited the monetary excesses of government by linking the domestic money supply more or less directly to available domestic reserves of gold, and thus allowed for an expansion in the money supply only following a period of overall surplus on the relevant current and capital accounts of the balance of payments. The second such rule, the balanced budget principle, limited the fiscal excesses of government by requiring governments to balance their expenditure outgoings, appropriately defined, with their taxation revenues save only during major wars.

During the 1930s the Gold Exchange Standard was swept away by the rival attempts of nation states to export their recessions to others *via* currency depreciation. Its post-war replacement was a system of fixed exchange rates which were adjusted frequently. The system finally collapsed during the early 1970s and was replaced by a flexible exchange-rate system. Throughout the post-war period, therefore, and increasingly in the 1970s, governments shook off their chains—the UK more than most—wrought damage to their economies, and endangered democracy by repeatedly debasing the currency in attempts to purchase increased output through unanticipated inflation.

Keynesian deficit economics and inflation

Since the Second World War, successive British governments have adopted the central message of Keynes that economies were led by aggregate demand rather than by aggregate supply and that fiscal imbalance was acceptable in pursuit of full-employment output. In the view of Keynes, such a shift of emphasis carried with it no long-term implications for public expenditure, since the excesses induced by recession would be redressed by the exigencies imposed by boom. In practice, of course, long-term fiscal balance has not occurred;

the post-war period has been rather one of chronic fiscal deficit, irrespective of the business cycle.

The reasons why unfettered governments tend to pursue policies of currency debasement and fiscal deficit are to be found within the institutional pressures of public choice. Over the limited period of an incumbent government, raising taxes and/or cutting public expenditure in real terms creates identifiable losers among the electorate, without a corresponding number of equally identifiable gainers. The adverse implications of deficit financing for rising inflation rates, rising interest rates and the relative advance of low-productivity public expenditure typically are reaped over periods longer than the British election cycle. The vote-motive[3] for fiscal deficits is evidently present.

In addition, the vulnerability of government, both central and local, to the budget deficit inevitably encourages the formation of groups whose principal *raison d'être* is that of lobbying successfully for resources from the public sector which would not be available within a competitive market system. Because of free-rider problems and widespread dispersion of benefits, consumer groups typically offer ineffectual defences when faced with well-organised rent-seeking producer groups which perceive direct and substantial benefits to themselves, albeit to the overall loss to society. As the public sector itself expands, and as public expenditure supports economically non-viable private sector projects, so is the vote-motive for deficit-financing extended and the pressure on governments to abjure fiscal conservatism re-inforced.

The existence of deficit-financing typically induces

[3] Gordon Tullock, *The Vote Motive*, Hobart Paperback **9**, IEA, 1976.

bureaucratic growth within the non-trading public sector, thus satisfying prime objectives within the bureaux. Thus it is that only the Treasury as a Department of British government is a defender of fiscal conservatism and that all other departments place excessive bids for resources, irrespective of the political beliefs of the (temporarily incumbent) Secretaries of State.

5. PUBLIC CHOICE AND THE MICRO-ECONOMIC FAILURE OF POST-WAR BRITISH GOVERNMENTS

The failure of post-war British governments to restrict public output to the provision of public goods has been noted. Thus, a trading public sector accounts for a significant proportion of gross domestic product. In principle, it is possible for public enterprises to achieve Pareto-efficiency. In practice, they have failed to do so in Britain, with consequential productivity losses, not least because public-choice pressures, vote-seeking and rent-seeking in nature, invaded the efficiency objectives, faced by only trivial consumer resistance.

Although the public trading corporations are confronted with financial targets, these have tended to be under-achieved with little political reaction. The aggregate losses of the nationalised industries have contributed to the overall deficit-financing of governments, and unjustifiable investment has been conceded for political ends, as in coal-mining, motor-cars and steel. The producer-group resistance to attempts at control has been successful, with cash limit after cash limit extended to avoid the closure of politically sensitive but highly unprofitable plant. There is no public equivalent to the private-sector capital market to discipline public corporations when government chooses to ignore the public-choice signals in favour of over-manning and low-productivity capital formation.

Bureaucracy out of control?

Within bureaucracy, the pressures of public choice tend to take a heavier toll in lost efficiency potential. In the absence of trading statistics, there is virtually no way of assessing either the economic desirability of particular budget allocations or the efficiency with which allocated budgets are utilised. Inevitably, such allocations become a focal point of political pressure, both *via* the vote mechanism and *via* well drilled rent-seeking operations. In response to budget cuts, senior bureaucrats have become skilled at implementing them to the maximum detriment of the voting public, thereby limiting the ability of vote-conscious governments to fulfil their election promises.

In general, British governments have proved particularly inept at controlling bureaucracy, especially by comparison with the USA where senior bureaucrats are expected to leave office with their defeated Executive and where inter-bureau competition is fostered. Nevertheless, Niskanen[4] has calculated that, even in the USA, bureaux outputs may be twice the size warranted by Paretian criteria and, moreover, are typically produced at a high cost in technical inefficiency.

The post-war British economy has been burdened not only with a large public sector but also with a vast

[4] W. A. Niskanen, *Bureaucracy and Representative Government*, Aldine-Atherton, Chicago, 1971, and *Bureaucracy: Servant or Master?*, Hobart Paperback 5, IEA, 1973

volume of legislation regulating the behaviour of private-sector corporations. Much of this legislation, laudable in its aims, is inimical to the fostering of an adaptive, competitive private-sector economy.

Regulation typically offers rents to those who are protected. The existence of rents induces socially wasteful rent-seeking activities both by outsiders and by the current beneficiaries. British governments still have not learnt that discrimination is best penalised and eliminated by fostering competition, both in the product and in the labour and capital markets. Nor have they yet learnt the message of Hayek that prosperous and free countries are the product, not of regulations rushed through the legislature into public law, but the outcome of centuries of common law development, with the courts reacting slowly but flexibly to assist the spontaneous order that a relatively unregulated economy fosters.

6. TOWARDS A PUBLIC CHOICE SOLUTION FOR THE UNITED KINGDOM

For the most part, British citizens do not enjoy the present economic environment of relative decline with all the conflict it fosters. Indeed, it is the widespread recognition that current policies represent a fundamental attempt to reverse such decline which allows the Conservative Government a lead in electoral opinion polls despite high unemployment. Whether such recognition will continue and, if so, with what eventual success, depends upon five main factors, all of which impinge on or help to shape the pattern of public choice in Britain.

(i) *Recognition of the limitations of government*

Recent experience in France, since the replacement of the Gaullist majority by the Mitterrand administration so closely followed the economic catastrophe in Britain from 1974 to 1976, has re-inforced growing public recognition that governments are no longer able to use inflation as a weapon against unemployment. Rises in government expenditure simply find their way into generalised inflation, to the advantage of the better-organised though not always the more productive rent-seekers, and into imports, with a consequential reduction in private capital formation and a limited fall in the currency exchange rate which itself also fuels inflation. Practical experience thus coincides with the developing literature of rational expectations[5] which strongly suggests that government actions generate neutralising changes within the structure of the economy as well-informed agents anticipate such moves and respond accordingly within the labour and product markets. Such growing individual recognition of the limited scope of government must be helpful to the development of a less governed, more individualistic society.

(ii) *The growth of private enterprise*

The decline of government in itself will not halt relative economic decline. It simply offers a potential which may or may not be seized, with an inevitable transition of apparent private-sector decline as firms accustomed to easy access to the public purse fail to survive the

[5] E.g., Patrick Minford, 'Restore Market Momentum and Fight On', in *Could Do Better*, IEA Occasional Paper Special, No. 62, IEA, 1982.

rigours of market forces. If, for 35 years or more, the brightest entrepreneurial talent has been lured into the public sector or into rent-seeking from the public sector, the process of transition may not be brief. That is the error in the Chicago model. Austrian economists have long reminded us that 'the animal spirits' necessary for entrepreneurial revival require a conducive economic climate and that de-regulation and privatisation of production and distribution is a *necessary* condition for that climate, but not a *sufficient* condition. There *is* an article of faith in the de-regulation/privatisation process. But there is a reasonable expectation that a nation as inventive and innovative as the British have been in the past will provide new products for domestic and international markets at prices which are competitive without government subsidy. Fortune will play its rôle. But zeal, far-sightedness and the instinct to survive should see the transition through this hazardous phase.

(iii) *Constitutional constraints on government*

Much has now been written about constitutional constraints upon government, but most of the literature relates to the USA with its *written* Constitution, both Federal and State. Within the USA, balanced-budget fiscal constraints are under serious consideration at both legislative levels to curb the fiscal deficits of successive vote-seeking Executives. The money supply has always been separately controlled by the Federal Reserve Bank, usually with a considerable degree of independence from any of the branches of government.

Britain is not yet ripe for such constitutional reform. Governments with absolute majorities will not curtail their powers *via* constitutions. In any event, the notion of Parliamentary sovereignty so deeply ingrained in

British political history makes it unlikely that a consti-tution voted in by one government would survive a simple majority vote of a hostile successor. Such solu-tions are an issue for, at best, a more consensual future.

(iv) *The federalisation of UK government*

Recent attempts at limited federalism for Wales and Scotland, initiated by the last Labour Government, failed not least because the federal proposals were limited geographically and offered little additional fiscal freedom to the two areas. Since 1979, a reverse process has been initiated whereby central government has strengthened its control over local governments by limiting their powers to ignore the Government's own financial and fiscal strategy.

For people who believe in freedom as well as for those who believe that inter-regional economic com-petition is conducive to national competitiveness, fiscal federalism is a welcome prospect, since individuals and firms are much more mobile between regions than between nations. Potential mobility of this kind acts as a severe constraint upon public authorities whose fiscal propensities are favourable to unproductive rent-seek-ing behaviour and unfavourable to output-conducive enterprise.

Fiscal federalism is not feasible within the present Parliament. It warrants serious consideration as a policy-issue by the next government, be it an absolute Conservative majority or a Conservative-Alliance coalition.

(v) *Proportional representation*

Proportional representation has been introduced by recent British governments both for elections to the

European Parliament and, more recently, to the Ulster
Assembly. Both Labour and Conservative governments, however, have persistently rejected such electoral
change when in office on a first-past-the-post absolute
majority of seats. Fears of permanent coalition per-
meate Westminster. The Liberal Party failed to force
proportional representation upon the failing Labour
Government as the price for supporting coalition during
the brief interim prior to the 1979 General Election.
Such opportunities are rarely offered by the British
electoral system.

However, the recent establishment of the Alliance
Party, together with forthcoming boundary changes,
may reduce the famous cube rule (whereby seat differences in the Commons tend to reflect the cube of vote
differences within the electorate) to the square rule
(similarly defined). If so, the prospect of an absolute
Conservative majority in the next election will be
diminished, though it must still remain the most likely
outcome. Any 'hung' Parliament may result in a policy
of proportional representation as the price of coalition.
In any event, even an absolute Conservative majority
would be wise to consider its introduction. For proportional representation represents a virtual guarantee
that collectivism will not be extended in Britain by the
political process.

7. CONCLUSIONS

The limits of the public choice perspective for the
reversal of economic decline in Britain have been outlined. The importance of this perspective cannot be
denied. But a central message of public choice is that

politicians themselves are severely constrained by the electorate and by the institutions they inherit. Only if the electorate is agreeable and the institutions receptive will the reversal of past trends be confirmed politically.

Adam Smith wrote that 'there is much Ruin in a nation'. Conversely, there is also fortitude, enterprise and individual productive endeavour. It is with a hope, indeed perhaps a belief, in the optimistic scenario for Britain that this paper ends.

BIBLIOGRAPHY

Arrow, K., *Social Choice and Individual Values*, Yale University Press, 1957.

Breton, A., *The Economics of Representative Government*, Aldine-Atherton, Chicago, 1974.

Breton, A., and Scott, A., *The Economic Constitution of Federal States*, University of Toronto Press, 1978.

Buchanan, J., and Tullock, G., *The Calculus of Consent*, Ann Arbor, Michigan, 1962.

Buchanan, J., and Wagner, R. E., *Democracy in Deficit*, Academic Press, New York, 1977.

Buchanan, J., Tollison, R., and Tullock, G., *Towards a Theory of the Rent-Seeking Society*, Texas A & M University Press, 1980.

Downs, A., *An Economic Theory of Democracy*, Harper and Row, New York, 1957.

Hayek, F. A., *The Constitution of Liberty*, Routledge & Kegan Paul, London, and University of Chicago Press, Chicago, 1960.

Niskanen, W. A., *Bureaucracy and Representative Government*, Aldine-Atherton, Chicago, 1971.

——, *Bureaucracy: Servant or Master?*, Hobart Paperback 5, IEA, 1973.

Seldon, A. (ed.), *The Economics of Politics*, IEA Readings No. 18, IEA, 1978.

Tullock, G., *The Vote Motive*, Hobart Paperback 9, IEA, 1976.

NINE

BRITAIN'S INTERNATIONAL ECONOMIC POLICY

A. I. MacBean

University of Lancaster

The Author

ALASDAIR MACBEAN: Professor of Economics and a Pro-Vice-Chancellor of the University of Lancaster. He has also taught economics at the University of Glasgow, been a Research Associate at the University of Harvard and a visiting professor at the University of Michigan, Ann Arbor, USA. He has been a member of the Harvard University Development Advisory Service in Pakistan, an Economic Adviser to the Ministry of Overseas Development, and a consultant to several UN agencies, USAID, and a Select Committee of the House of Lords. He is the author of *Export Instability and Economic Development* (1966), (with V. N. Balasubramanyam), *Meeting the Third World Challenge* (1976, 2nd Edn. 1978) and *A Positive Approach to the International Economic Order* (1978), and (with P. N. Snowden), *International Institutions in Trade and Finance* (1981).

Britain's International Economic Policy

1. GOALS

What do the general aims of Social Democrats imply for the objectives of international economic policy for Britain? All mainstream political parties accept efficiency, equity and economic growth as the principal social objectives. Where they differ is in the relative importance they attach to these goals and in the means by which they think the goals can be achieved.

The main areas of international economic policy are trade in goods and services, flows of capital, labour and technology, issues of balance of payments and exchange rates, attitudes to the European Community, other OECD nations, the Third World and the centrally planned economies of Eastern Europe, attitudes to the main international institutions such as the General Agreement on Tariffs and Trade (GATT) and the International Monetary Fund (IMF). What should be the policies of Social Democrats in these areas?

Free trade, free markets

For many reasons Social Democrats should be strong proponents of free international trade. They want decentralised decision-making, power to the people, less bureaucracy but more international co-operation.[1]

[1] These views of what some Social Democrats stand for can be found in the SDP 'Application for Founder Membership of the SDP', 1981, and in John Horam, 'Discussion Paper, Economic Policy', SDP, 2 July 1981.

These are all powerful arguments for aiming at reducing barriers to international trade. For most of the economic decisions which have to be made, the most decentralised system of decision-making possible is a free market. Provided that it operates under workable competitive conditions its great virtue is that it combines efficiency with freedom for buyers and sellers to act on their own views as to what is in their best interests. It is also in general an efficient system because, for familiar reasons, a free market leads firms to produce what consumers want at the lowest possible cost. But to be efficient a market needs to function without monopoly or collusion among sellers or buyers. It also requires that information on quality and prices should be easy and cheap to obtain. This enables people, within their budget limits, to buy their requirements at the lowest cost and to sell their products and services to the highest bidders. This has to be a powerful argument for free trade since it vastly increases the size of the market. By bringing in many more producers and consumers, free trade must weaken national monopolies and considerably increases the difficulty of collusion to rig markets by increasing both numbers of participants and sources of information.

Over the long run, efficiency in the use of our resources requires that we import goods wherever the cost of producing those goods for ourselves exceeds the cost of producing other goods which can be exchanged for the imports. This is easily accepted when we exchange engineering products for rice or cocoa, but some find it less convincing when we simultaneously import BMW or Alfa Romeo cars and export Jaguars and Triumphs. But much trade nowadays is among the developed countries and in finished manufactures.

Reasons for this lie in the increasing sophistication of relatively affluent consumers who demand a wide variety of products from which to pick those which meet most nearly their precise requirements, and in the importance of economies of scale in the production of durable consumer goods. The consumers' liking for variety can be met at much lower cost through trade than by each nation's firms trying to produce such a variety in necessarily shorter production runs for themselves.

Benefits of trade v. costs of protection

The complexity and specialisation of equipment in production processes provides a similar explanation for the large volume of trade in intermediate goods and machinery. But trade in similar goods has further justifications. It promotes competition, forcing firms to keep on their toes, to keep down costs, to pay attention to consumers' preferences and to provide good back-up services for their products. A captive home market protected by tariffs or quotas soon breeds complacency, mounting inefficiency and contempt for customers. It also significantly strengthens the bargaining position of trade unions in such industries. The damage inflicted upon themselves by high protection of domestic industry has been well-documented in a number of studies of developing countries in the last 15 years.[2] The frus-

[2] I. Little, T. Scitovsky and M. Scott, *Industry and Trade in Some Developing Countries,* Oxford University Press, 1970; Bela Balassa, *The Newly Industrialising Countries in the World Economy*, Pergamon Press, 1981; Jagdish Bhagwati, *Foreign Trade Régimes and Economic Development: Anatomy and Consequences of Exchange Control Régimes*, Ballinger, Cambridge, Mass., 1978; Anne Krueger, *Foreign Trade Régimes and Economic Development: Liberalisation Attempts and Consequences*, Ballinger, Cambridge, Mass., 1978.

trations and the inefficiencies widespread in the highly autarkic nations of Eastern Europe are common knowledge.

Trade theories such as the 'protection and real wages argument' suggest some situations where free trade would raise the rate of profit and lower the real wage. Pragmatism can point to groups of workers whose jobs will be lost and incomes reduced by free trade. But does free trade generally promote more equality of incomes? This is a difficult question to answer because it depends upon circumstances. But in today's world most protection worsens the distribution of income between nations and probably also makes incomes less equal within nations. At best it is an inefficient way of supporting the incomes of domestic producers.

The highest levels of protection are in agriculture in the relatively rich industrial nations. But the worst effects fall on poor nations whose exports of raw and refined sugar, beef, veal, coffee, wine, tobacco and maize are held down both in quantity and price by OECD nations' policies of protecting agriculture. Within the OECD nations, consumers' real incomes are reduced since they pay higher prices than they need for agricultural products while most of the benefits accrue in the form of increased land values and higher land rents.[3] Since food is a major item in the budget of most poor people, the probability is that protection in OECD countries has transferred income from relatively poor people to the relatively rich. It has probably not

---

[3] D. Gale Johnson, *World Agriculture in Disarray*, Macmillan, 1973, and A. Valdes and J. Zietz, 'Agricultural Protection in OECD Countries: Its Cost to Less-Developed Countries', Research Report for the International Food Policy Research Institute, Washington DC, December 1980.

done much to help poor farmers in the OECD nations[4] and, insofar as it has, that objective could have been met at a lower social cost by direct income transfers or a deficiency payments system for farm prices. It is in theory possible to design protection to re-distribute income in favour of poor people, but few governments have done so. In any case, direct transfers through taxes and subsidies could do the job better.

Free trade and economic growth

Does free trade promote growth? At the least, since it raises current national incomes, it raises the ability of economies to save and invest. But more than this: it exposes their businessmen to new ideas and new technologies and by widening markets enables industries to exploit economies of scale to the fullest extent.

Once again some arguments for protection have attained a degree of respectability—the 'terms of trade argument for tariffs' or 'protection for infant industries', for example. But the first of these is a beggar-my-neighbour policy which invites retaliation and the second a much overdone argument for government intervention. Even when new industry can be identified as likely to be a major success yet for some reason cannot attract sufficient private backing, protection by tariff or quota is likely to be the least efficient form of government help. A subsidy financed from general taxation would be superior.[5]

[4] D. Gale Johnson, *op. cit.*

[5] Harry G. Johnson, 'Optimal trade intervention in the presence of domestic distortions', in Jagdish Bhagwati (ed.), *International Trade*, Penguin Modern Economics, Penguin Books, 1969.

The general predilection of Social Democrats on all three counts—efficiency, equity and growth—is that free trade is best for the world as a whole and for Britain as a whole. Of course, any specific reduction in trade barriers or change in our relative advantages in production *vis à vis* other nations involves our economy in changes which will benefit some and hurt others. Social democrats would surely wish to ease the process of adjustment to trade-induced change and to make sure that those who suffer through no fault of their own should be compensated and given help to re-train.

The general assumption that progressive movement towards free international trade is a highly desirable goal will affect Social Democrats' views on a whole set of policy issues: attitudes to the European Community, the developing countries and particularly the newly industrialising countries (NICs), and to a series of controversial issues hotly debated in the General Agreement on Tariffs and Trade (GATT) which will be discussed in the section on British policies.

2. CONSTRAINTS ON BRITISH POLICIES

Britain's international economic situation is bedevilled by a number of problems, some of them long-term and deep-seated in nature. These impose severe constraints on what governments can do. No instant solutions are possible, but policies to overcome these problems are essential. Constraints are also imposed by the situation of the rest of the world. World recession, energy costs, deflationary policies in most OECD nations, financial crises in several major developing nations and some centrally planned economies represent the other main constraints on policies to-day. We also have obligations in the European Community and as members of the GATT and the IMF which could rule out some policies.

Britain's declining exports of manufactures

In 1899 Britain accounted for about 32 per cent of world exports of manufactures. Today the figure is about 10 per cent.[6] We used to export manufactures and import mainly food and raw materials. Now 63 per cent of imports are manufactures or semi-manufactures. Between 1970 and 1980 our manufactured exports increased by 52 per cent in volume, but over the same period our imports of manufactures increased by 132 per cent.[7] The relative profitability of exporting manufactures from the UK has declined in recent years, and so has the ability of our industries to compete on price with imports.[8] Various estimates suggest that a given increase in UK income produces about double the increase in volume of imports which a similar percentage increase in income for the rest of the world produces in demand for our exports. It should be noted that most of these changes took place before North Sea oil started to make a significant impact on Britain's balance of payments.

The decline in Britain's share in world manufacturing

[6] J. S. Metcalfe, 'Foreign trade and the balance of payments', in A. R. Prest and D. J. Coppock, *The UK Economy*, Weidenfeld and Nicolson, 1982, pp. 142-3.

[7] The Claire Group, 'Problems of Industrial Recovery', *Midland Bank Review*, Spring 1982, p. 10.

[8] CSO, *Economic Trends*, August 1982, p. 46. Here 1983 has seen some improvement.

cannot be shrugged off as simply a natural adaptation to catching-up on Britain's initial lead by the rest of the world. We are a small, trade-dependent (exports remain 30 per cent of GDP), densely populated island whose prosperity depends on our ability to use our skills productively. North Sea oil has a strict time-limit as a life preserver. If we cannot make a comeback in manufacturing we shall have to accept a severe reduction in relative living standards—and it is extremely difficult to see how we should be able to provide our population with the jobs they want. Although the services sector is very large in the national economy and will continue to grow, exports of services are only one-third of exports of goods.

The reasons for the tremendous increase in import penetration in manufacturing and our weakness in exports seem to be a combination of relative costs and a series of non-price factors such as failures to maintain quality, reliability on delivery, selling and after-sales services, lack of speed in developing new products and adjusting to change. The cost/price factors can be identified to a reasonable extent, the others are more difficult to quantify. Since the early 1950s Britain's growth rate and rate of increase in labour productivity have lagged behind those of our rivals in trade. Since our exchange rate remained fixed and over-valued for long periods, profit margins were squeezed in export markets. Wages went on rising because of high levels of demand through the 1970s. As trade in manufactures became freer with the various rounds of tariff cuts and with membership of the EEC, import penetration rose sharply. Low profits in British manufacturing led to low investment in new products, new equipment, research and development. Thus was created a vicious circle in which manufacturing industry in Britain necessarily became less progressive and less competitive.[9]

The dilemma for economic policy

More recently, a combination of the real and psychological impact of North Sea oil, together with the tough monetary policies of the Thatcher Government and high interest rates, pushed up the exchange value of sterling to a level which seriously handicapped British manufacturers in competition with foreigners. This high exchange rate has been a key cause of unemployment levels in Britain which have been on average higher than in other major industrial nations, but it has also helped to keep down import prices and dampen inflation. Clearly there is a dilemma here for economic policy.

The scope for independent macro-economic policies in a country as dependent as Britain is upon the rest of the world is rather limited. Over 30 per cent of our GDP is exported and imports also amount to more than 30 per cent of GDP. Whatever we do affects our trading partners and whatever they do affects us. Apart from trade there is also the influence of capital movements which may swing violently between nations in response to actual or rumoured changes in interest or exchange rates.

Given these constraints, what policies are available for Social Democrats to pursue today?

[9] NEDO, *International Price Competitiveness, Non-Price Factors and Export Performance*, HMSO, 1977. The real rate of profit on capital employed in manufacturing industry fell from about 12 per cent in 1960 to around 3 per cent in the late 1970s. (G. Maynard, 'Micro-economic Deficiencies in UK Macro-economic Policy', *Lloyds Bank Review*, July 1982.)

3. POLICIES

Britain's major weakness lies in trade in manufactures. In recent years this has been masked by a contribution from oil and gas to the balance of payments of about £10 billion and by the constraint upon imports stemming from depressed aggregate demand. Social Democrats would presumably wish to expand demand at home to raise the profitability of industry, expand output, stimulate investment and create jobs. However this is done, past experience indicates that there would be a sharp rise in imports. The consequent further depreciation in the exchange rate is likely to give a further twist to inflation. Econometric work suggests on past experience that a 10 per cent depreciation would directly raise retail prices by 2·5 per cent within two years, but allowing for repercussions upon wage bargains the full effect would be 9 per cent in two to four years and eventually the full competitive gain from the depreciation of the exchange rate would be wiped out by a full 10 per cent increase in domestic prices.[10]

Difficulties of international co-operation

An obvious way of avoiding or reducing the exchange rate depreciation would be if our main trading partners could be induced to expand their economies at the same time. Such international co-operation would certainly commend itself to Social Democrats. But three drawbacks should be noted:

(1) If all the industrial nations were to expand their

[10] M. Panic, 'Monetarism in an Open Economy', *Lloyds Bank Review*, July 1982, p. 39, based on Bank of England Discussion Paper No. 8, London, 1980.

economies quickly by a significant amount, current oil surpluses could be mopped up and increases in oil prices become likely.

(2) There would be bottlenecks in the supply of other primary commodities and raw materials which would push up their prices.

(3) Even although there is widespread unemployment and excess capacity, expansion could hit against specific bottlenecks such as shortages of workers with special skills.

These risks argue for expanding demand gradually on a combined basis. But fears of inflation, differences in timing of elections and other factors militate against the international co-operative approach. If Britain wishes to expand faster than the rest of the world, how should it be done?

Powerful voices on the Left, the TUC, substantial sections of the Labour Party and the Cambridge Economic Policy Group (CEPG), all argue that the way out of the dilemma is the imposition of general import controls. The CEPG has consistently argued from 1975 onwards that the only way to salvage Britain's manufacturing industry and restore employment is through expanding domestic demand and preventing imports from rising by high tariffs or exchange controls bearing generally upon all manufactures.[11] There is no space in this short essay to set out the arguments and counter-arguments fully. (For that readers should see the CEPG's own presentations and the *Case Against General Import Restrictions* by M. Fg.

---

[11] CEPG, *Cambridge Economic Policy Review*, February 1975, and subsequent annual reviews to date.

Scott, W. M. Corden and Ian Little.)[12] But it is evident that to follow that line would be in breach of the Rome Treaty, and our membership of the GATT. Import controls would run serious risks of retaliation, and could be as inflationary if not more so than depreciation. If controls were maintained for only a few years they would probably not induce the desired investment in manufacturing, and if kept on longer would lead to serious inefficiencies. They would in any case militate against exports by sucking them back into the domestic market and pulling resources away from them. Social Democrats are unlikely to be attracted by these proposals.

A cautious expansion?

What they could settle for is a moderate expansion of demand through easier monetary and fiscal policies which would lead to some depreciation of the exchange rate combined with an incomes policy designed to prevent earnings rising faster than productivity. The evaluation of the crucial element, the incomes policy, is examined elsewhere in this collection, but in my view, despite weaknesses in past attempts to control incomes, the situation today holds out much higher hopes of success. Unemployment will remain very high during the first two to three years of expanding output, thus weakening union bargaining power in the private sector. Productivity is likely to rise fast initially as output expands, making some real-wage increases possible without raising prices. Public sector wage restraints are already in force and normally wages there follow private sector wage increases with a one- to two-year

[12] Thames Essay No. 24, Trade Policy Research Centre, 1980.

lag. Inflationary expectations are being adjusted down-wards as high unemployment and world recession have checked the rate of increase in prices and earnings.

Resistance to the growth of protectionism would help both to dampen inflation in the UK by giving consumers access to cheaper goods and aid employ-ment by giving higher incomes to other countries, particularly the NICs, to buy our exports. One could expect Social Democrats to support policies to liberalise the Multi-Fibres Arrangement and to use their influence in the GATT to resist the growth of non-tariff barriers to imports from the developing countries.[13] An economy like Britain's is dependent on exporting manufactures, but manufacturing, as it becomes routine, is more cheaply based in countries with lower labour costs combining with standard technology so that it moves to the NICs. Britain then must continually move up-market into goods and marketable services containing more skill, more technology and higher quality. If we do not keep adjusting, our living standards are bound to fall far behind the front-rank nations. We are too small to 'go it alone' behind tariff walls. We must become more efficient or reconcile ourselves to relative poverty once the oil runs out.

While supporting continued British membership of the European Community, one should also expect Social Democrats to wish to wean the Community away from its heavy protection of agriculture. Quite apart from the higher cost of food and the fiscal and

[13] Donald Keesing and Martin Wolf, *Textile Quotas against Developing Countries*, Thames Essay No. 23, Trade Policy Research Centre, 1980; M. Scott *et al.*, *op. cit.*; R. Blackhurst, N. Marian, J. Tumlir, *Trade Liberalisation, Protectionism and Interdependence*, GATT Secretariat, 1977.

exchange burdens inflicted on Britain by the Common Agriculture Policy (CAP), agricultural exporting nations such as Australia, New Zealand, North America and many developing countries are hurt by it. The intellectual case for reform, based on efficiency and equity, is irrefutable. The main obstacle is quirks in the electoral systems and internal balance of power in France and Germany. A gradual shift to a deficiency payments system for support to agricultural incomes is probably the best hope of rationalising the system, but it is a long-term hope at best.

The pros and cons of exchange controls

A tricky issue is the question of exchange controls over capital movements. Short-term capital movements often produce swings in exchange rates which serve no useful purpose in terms of effecting resource switches between activities. They merely increase the exchange risks of transacting business. Up to a point central banks can cope with such short-term capital flows by offsetting movements in reserves and net official borrowing so as to maintain reasonable stability in exchange rates. Also up to a point firms can hedge foreign exchange transactions by offsetting purchases or sales of currency in the forward markets. Nevertheless it remains likely that much short-term capital flows impose costs on the economy. Does this represent a convincing argument for a restoration of exchange controls over capital movements by British citizens? Probably not. Experience during the era of pegged exchange rates and official capital controls showed that merely by leading or lagging payments on commercial transactions, enormous sums of money could be taken in or out of

Britain in anticipation of changes in the value of sterling.

Is there a case for controls on the ground of the effects on long-term direct investment? In recent years British companies and private citizens have been investing heavily abroad. Socialists have blamed this on the removal of exchange controls by the Conservative Government in 1979. But even supposing controls had been maintained, would this have benefitted our economy? The evidence suggests that profit rates in British industry were too low to attract such capital. Many overseas investments would have been permitted as necessary defensive or internationally strategic measures by British firms. Determined investors would in many cases have found ways around the controls. Land, property, the financial sector and government stocks would presumably have provided homes for some of the frustrated overseas investments with perhaps some increase in consumption. Our exchange rate would have been somewhat higher, thus increasing our economic difficulties. It is doubtful that there is much case for a re-introduction of foreign exchange controls on British citizens.

4. CONCLUSION

The main message for Social Democrats is to pursue free trade as far as possible. Where this results in inequitable burdens or loss of income and need to redeploy labour, Social Democrats may recognise a need to slow down import penetration temporarily but they should recognise that adjustment, whether to changes in trade or technology, is essential to our future prosperity. Society should provide easy access to re-training for new jobs and every assistance and encouragement to take advantage of such opportunities. Where necessary, 'fair' compensation should be given to workers who through no fault of their own cannot be found alternative employment.[14]

[14] A. I. MacBean and P. N. Snowden, *International Institutions in Trade and Finance*, Allen and Unwin, 1981, pp. 241-4.